T

K E E L E
UNIVERSITY **LIBRARY**

Please return by the last date or time shown

POLITICS AND PAINTING
Murals and Conflict in Northern Ireland

POLITICS AND PAINTING
Murals and Conflict in Northern Ireland

BILL ROLSTON

Rutherford • Madison • Teaneck
Fairleigh Dickinson University Press
London and Toronto: Associated University Presses

Associated University Presses
440 Forsgate Drive
Cranbury, NJ 08512

Associated University Presses
25 Sicilian Avenue
London WC1A 2QH, England

Associated University Presses
P.O. Box 39, Clarkson Pstl. Stn.
Mississauga, Ontario,
L5J 3X9 Canada

Library of Congress Cataloging-in-Publication Data

Rolston, Bill.
   Politics and painting : murals and conflict in Northern Ireland /
Bill Rolston.
      p.   cm.
   Includes bibliographical references.
   ISBN 0-8386-3386-2 (alk. paper)
   1. Mural painting and decoration, Irish—Northern Ireland.
   2. Mural painting and decoration—20th century—Northern Ireland.
   3. Street art—Northern Ireland.   I. Title.
ND2737.A3N657   1991
751.7'3'094160904—dc20   89-45981
                                                                              CIP

The paper used in this publication meets the requirements of the American National Standard for Permanence of Paper for Printed Library Materials Z39.48-1984.

PRINTED IN THE UNITED STATES OF AMERICA

For Anna,
who believed that this book would
eventually be produced,
even when I didn't

and for Nalina,
aged four,
who likes colors.

Contents

Foreword

As an artist working in the fine art tradition, I have always been frustrated by the commonly held belief that this particular approach to the production of images can only expect a narrow and often exclusive audience, and also that it is not the business of ordinary people. I have felt disinclined to accept this view and consequently have striven over many years to make my images accessible to as wide an audience as possible.

Therefore, to communicate my ideas I use a visual language that has been in common currency for more than five hundred years and consequently readily accepted by most people as a truthful way to depict reality; conversely, I have avoided the excesses of the avant garde because, in my opinion, they can inhibit popular cognition. I frequently have used reproduction to reach beyond the narrow audience of the gallery-dealer-critic system; for, as Berger (1972: 32) argues, "images can now be ephemeral, ubiquitous, insubstantial, available, valueless, free." I suppose what I have been striving for is the condition described, with some accuracy, by Glyn Banks in 1982 as that in which "the artist is seen not as an alienated visionary or formalist researcher into visual knowledge but primarily as someone who gives expression to what is common knowledge." Yet I must confess that, in spite of my best efforts, I have failed more often than succeeded. I still feel that my work frequently exists in a context that is irrelevant to the lives of most people.

Of course, there are those who argue that this is inevitable because the majority have no use for any form of art in their daily struggle. I am unwilling to accept this proposition, however, and I believe that the development of the political wall paintings in Northern Ireland during recent years reinforces my rejection. I am especially interested in the explosion of wall painting in nationalist areas during the 1981 hunger strike that began on the morning of 1 March when Bobby Sands, the republican prisoners' leader, refused his breakfast. Outside the prison, republican activists organized local committees to win support for the hunger strike. Initially walls in nationalist areas were covered with graffiti urging support for the hunger strikers, then images related to the struggle slowly began to be introduced. By this time the hunger strike was receiving massive attention from both national and international news media, particularly with the parliamentary election of Bobby Sands; however, after his death a real sense of anxiety grew within the nationalist community as the worldwide blaze of publicity faded. At this stage the ordinary people of the nationalist areas turned with increased enthusiasm to painting, a medium that, we are told constantly, is irrelevant to their lives.

I find it fascinating that people with little previous aesthetic experience turned to a specific visual art form to tell their own story and to reinforce their determination to continue their struggle against injustice. Art rarely becomes a common point of reference for a social group in that it helps form their political and cultural ideas and articulates their ideals.

As an artist who constantly struggles against alienation and marginalization, yet who frequently feels estranged from ordinary life, I admit to a pang of envy for these mostly anonymous artists whose work is central to the social and cultural life of their own community and which forms a crucial weapon of resistance in the struggle against oppression and injustice.

Dublin   ROBERT BALLAGH
February 1989

Acknowledgments

Thanks are due to the following for permission to rephotograph their original photographs for inclusion in this book: *Belfast Telegraph;* Central Library, Belfast; Anna Eggert; Paddy Hillyard; Marilyn and Dave Hyndman; Linenhall Library, Belfast; Siobhan Molloy; *Newsletter,* Belfast; Northern Ireland Information Service; Elaine Thomas; Daniel Wasson.

For permission to quote from his poem "Letter to a British Soldier on Irish Soil," Patrick Galvin.

For help in locating murals and photographs of murals: Liz Curtis, Anna Eggert, Jim Ledwith, Fred Heatley, Belinda Loftus, Roisin McDonough, Noel McGuigan, Gerry Moore, Jack Myers, Marie Smyth, Julian Watson.

For more general assistance, including those who agreed to be interviewed: Joe Coyle, Digger, Gerard Kelly, Kes, Ray McCullough, Yvonne McCullough, David Simpson, Paul Parkhill, librarians at the University of Ulster, librarians at the Linenhall Library.

Above all, thanks to Tony Feenan of the University of Ulster for countless hours of work in producing excellent prints from often poor originals.

POLITICS AND PAINTING
Murals and Conflict in Northern Ireland

1
Triumph and Confusion: Loyalist Wall Murals

FROM PLANTATION TO STATE

"REMEMBER 1690" IS PERHAPS THE MOST EMOTIVE slogan of Unionism. The date has mythical, almost mystical importance. In that year the Protestant King William of Orange is said to have stopped the Catholic attempt to reestablish royal power in England by beating Catholic King James at the Battle of the Boyne in Ireland and then occupying the English throne. His victory, it is said, guaranteed Protestant liberty rather than Catholic authoritarianism in both England and Ireland. As a watershed in Protestant history, particularly Irish Protestant, the significance of the year 1690 is stamped indelibly on the Protestant collective consciousness in Ireland.

The perceived importance of the event is not marred by the countering of myth with some uncomfortable facts. For example, given the balance of political forces in Western Europe at the time, it was Protestant William rather than Catholic James who had the pope's blessing in the battle. Moreover, there were Protestants serving in the Jacobite forces, just as there were Catholics among William's troops. Although celebrated traditionally on the Twelfth of July each year, the battle actually occurred on 1 July, the later date change resulting from Britain's late

adoption of the Gregorian calendar. Moreover, the Battle of the Boyne apparently was not much more than a prolonged skirmish, the more decisive battle being at Aughrim the following year; neither William nor James was present at the latter battle.

Finally, and perhaps most significantly, William's success did not guarantee liberty for *all* Irish Protestants. Protestant planters, settled in the northern part of Ireland in the early seventeenth century, had experienced a precarious existence. Having ousted the native Catholics to occupy land, they found themselves beleaguered, at no time more obviously than in 1641, when the Irish rose up and came close to razing the plantation towns. Despite the common enemy, however, the planters were themselves divided along class and religious lines. The gentry were for the most part Anglican, while the peasantry was Presbyterian. Anglicans feared the dissenting radicalism of the Presbyterians and attempted to ensure that Presbyterianism, if not suppressed, was at least politically curtailed. Presbyterians may have hoped that their allegiance to the Williamite cause would bring them political recognition in Ireland. But, although William himself did show his gratitude in some ways (such as the renewal of the custom of *regium donum*, the royal grant for the Presbyterian Church), Anglicans in Ireland made sure that Presbyterianism continued to be curtailed politically for much of the eighteenth century. This fact more than any other led sections of the Presbyterian middle class to become a revolutionary force at the end of the century. Judging themselves blocked economically and politically by the Anglicans, they found common cause with the Catholic peasantry in the United Irishmen revolution of 1798.

The abject failure of that revolution paradoxically led to the emergence of a system wherein the Presbyterian middle class found the obstacles to their political and economic progress removed. The Act of Union of 1801, despite being a punishment for revolutionary activity, gave the middle class the niche it sought, but not within an Irish economy. The link with Britain became all important to emerging Presbyterian industrialists (and by extension to the Protestant workers employed by them), thus guaranteeing the end of their brief flirtation with secessionist aspirations. It was the Catholics, of whatever class, who continued to advocate secession from British influence, albeit differing on the means to achieve that end.

Given the Act of Union, the basis existed for a cessation of old rivalries among the planters. An alliance of the different Protestant classes provided advantages for each of the classes involved. Despite major differences of class interest, ideology, and politics, the alliance forged at the turn of the nineteenth century proved remarkably sturdy in the years that followed.

The complexity of the alliance, the balance of fragility and stability, can be illustrated by a brief consideration of what was for long the backbone of the alliance, the Orange Order. The late eighteenth century saw the growth of many peasant secret societies in Ireland. Many existed to carry out actions against exploitative or absentee landlords. In the north, however, a strong element of sectarianism emerged. One Protestant peasant group, the Peep O' Day Boys, derived their name from their practice of raiding Catholic homes at dawn and searching for weapons that Catholics were forbidden by law to possess. In response,

Catholic peasants banded together in a large group called the Defenders and defeated the Protestants at the Battle of the Diamond in County Armagh in 1795. After that defeat the Protestant peasant societies amalgamated as the Orange Society, later named the Orange Order. As a peasant group with some roots in agrarian class action, the Orange Order was not initially viewed with sympathy by the gentry. On the other hand, the Order's existence proved opportune in the aftermath of the United Irishmen rebellion of 1798. The gentry used the Orange Order as its main counter-revolutionary force (Gibbon 1975). When that crisis, and the later, smaller rebellion of Robert Emmet in 1803 passed, the hostility between gentry and peasantry returned. The Orange Order was banned between 1836 and 1868 but was revived later to become the backbone of unionist resistance to British moves, beginning in the 1880s to grant Home Rule to Ireland.

As the rise and fall of the Orange Order shows, despite its fragility, the overall trend was toward alliance rather than disintegration. Indeed, it also is clear that there is no unbroken and even line of stability stretching right back to the "glorious victory" of 1690, nor a clear cultural continuity stretching back without fault or blemish for three centuries. The Orange Order emerged a full century after William's victory and was not fully established as the backbone of the unionist alliance until a century after that. Similarly, the symbols of unionist unity were not always nor equally shared by each of the classes participating in the alliance. Indeed, there is partial continuity. As Loftus (1980a, p. 3) notes, the standard contemporary image of King William as a heroic historical figure on horseback at the Battle of the Boyne originated in a painting by Benjamin West, first exhibited in 1780. Although probably never exhibited in Ireland, the painting became the basis for engravings that did become relatively popular in Ireland, appearing in collections of loyalist songs or printed on silk handkerchiefs. However, the historical hero image of William was not the first to appear. Loftus (1977, p. 8) explains:

In the representations of William produced during his lifetime, he was shown in two main roles. . . . Either he was a timeless, classical emperor, or a historical, heroic leader, often mounted on horse-back and leading his troops into battle. The first was a long-standing cliche, which went back to the Roman emperors, and had become particularly popular following the Renaissance revival of classical imagery. The second was relatively new, probably developed by the Dutch. . . . The Roman emperor image predominated at first.

Thus as early as ten years after the Battle of the Boyne, a "Roman emperor" statue of William was erected outside Trinity College Dublin[1] (where it remained until 1929). But the heroic, historical William was the one that appealed more to the northern gentry. As Loftus (1980a, p. 3) puts it, "for them identification with the equestrian victor was a means of enforcing their own aura of leadership." With the emergence of cheap forms of mass production of images in the twentieth century, it was the by then well-established William the historical hero, rather than William the timeless semideity, who appeared on postcards and the like.

In short, the forging of the political alliance between various classes of Protestants in the north meant the "victory" of one representation over another. Later, the strengthening of that alliance in the struggle against Home Rule guaranteed cultural certainty and the wider acceptance of what were by then traditional images. Similarly, Loftus (1980a, p. 1) claims that "much of their gorgeous paraphernalia of banners, sashes and street arches" originated with the establishment of the Orange Order, but with the Home Rule crisis from the 1880s they became truly established as the very essence of unionist solidarity. Differing slightly from Loftus, Hayes-McCoy (1979, p. 171) underlines more emphatically that political solidarity brought with it more contemporary cultural certainty:

> In the early days of the Order the Orangemen appear to have marched behind flags rather than banners. The Orange banners which we now know and which have preserved in a remarkable manner the characteristic mid-19th century form of the painted double-sided banner borne between two poles are probably no older than the 1880s.

THE TRIUMPH OF UNIONISM: THE NORTHERN IRELAND STATE

Just as each section of the Protestant alliance derived different benefits from unity, so each had a different role to play in the alliance—the aristocracy and businessmen as "generals," the peasantry and working class as "foot soldiers." The alliance continued to be uneasy, with the followers often threatening to bypass the leadership in sectarian militance or their opposition to economic exploitation at the hands of the dominant classes, or, apparently paradoxically, in terms of both at once. But the alliance showed its power and efficiency in relation to the successful opposition against a series of three Home Rule Bills between 1886 and 1912. As the third Home Rule Bill appeared to be heading for success, the unionist bourgeoisie and gentry formed a government-in-waiting and placed themselves at the head of illegally organized units of a mass loyalist army, the Ulster Volunteer Force (UVF). The tactic worked; major sections of the British establishment, including senior army officers, colluded with the unionists in activity that was treasonable. Other sections of the British bourgeoisie did not wish to impose Home Rule on the whole of Ireland against the firm will of a majority of people in one small part of Ireland; partition seemed the easy solution to this dilemma. Even those in the British establishment who were sympathetic to Home Rule lacked the courage to take on such a formidable alliance; their lack of initiative contributed to the emergence of partition. World War I interrupted the Home Rule momentum, and this was followed by the War of Independence in the south and west of Ireland. In 1921, partition was imposed and the Northern Ireland state was formed. Those who had constituted the provisional government in the north a few years previously took over the reins of state power without firing a single shot against the British establishment.

The formation of the state institutionalized and legitimized not only the unionist alliance, but also all the symbols and cultural definitions forged and accepted by that alliance. Patently sectional symbols such as flags, banners, arches, songs, marches, and other events took on the aura of universality; party emblems expanded to civic proportions. All of this was built, as we shall see in chapter 3, on the exclusion of a large minority of the population, the Catholics/nationalists, from power and the process of defining the symbols and cultural discourse of the state. The state and its legitimacy rested on the triumph of unionism over nationalism, with essential British cooperation, in one part of Ireland.

The state itself was of course the overarching symbol of that triumph, an institution whose very existence proclaimed the supposed legitimacy of unionist victory, a legitimacy rejected or at least seriously questioned by a sizeable proportion of its citizens. The legitimacy of the other civic symbols flowed from the establishment of the state and also broadcast a triumphalist message.

This is not to say that sectarianism and all the other hallmarks of triumphalism were or are foremost in the consciousness of everyone who ever marched on the Twelfth of July or recognized the Union Jack as the "national" flag or "God save the King/Queen" as the "national" anthem. Thus, in 1961 Jack Loudan probably summed up that consciousness accurately:

> I have watched the young people, the boys and the girls who are out for the day and who have, I always think, no real awareness of any historical or political significance behind the event. This is their day out—and they intend to enjoy it.

However, even purely cultural manifestations are never solely apolitical, but contain a triumphalist message, even if on occasions it is slightly veiled. Buckley (1986), for example, attempts to explain the consciousness of men who play the huge and noisy loyalist Lambeg drums in one part of County Antrim:

> The Lambeg drum in this case was indeed affirming a distinctly Protestant identity; but it was also doing something else. It was asserting the values . . . of "plainness," masculinity, straightforwardness, bluntness and good fellowship. . . .

Because such values are seen by the musicians to be uniquely and exclusively Protestant, they emphasize that the triumphalism is never far below the surface of apparently harmless

cultural events. Lambeg drum playing may not be intended directly as anti-Catholic activity, but that is ultimately part of the message in the exclusivist attitudes of these players.

Similarly, a Church of Ireland lay preacher, speaking at the annual march of the loyalist Apprentice Boys in Derry in 1987, could specifically reject the accusation that the march was triumphalist, and also condescendingly reveal that participation in the event demands a theological commitment of Apprentice Boys that is exclusively Protestant.

> We can say to our Catholic neighbours we are not better than you. Indeed, despite what we believe to be serious errors of doctrine in your Church, if you have repented of your sin and if you trust in the *finished work* of Jesus at Calvary, then you are our brothers in Christ, *irrespective of your culture and irrespective of your political outlook.* (emphasis mine)[2]

In structural terms, therefore, despite the complexities and rationalizations of each individual's consciousness, the ritualistic parading of unionist symbols is and was inevitably triumphalist. The symbols presumed a consensus that did not exist, a facade preserved as much by force and fear as by sullen acceptance. As far as the nationalist minority was concerned, the very existence of the symbols as civic ones inevitably represented the triumph of unionism and the suppression of nationalism in the North of Ireland. Regardless of individual consciousness, the symbols declared the structural superiority of unionism.

The events of the Twelfth of July each year provide a case in point. The Twelfth is frequently depicted as no more than a carnival-like event. Similar to Bastille Day in France or Independence Day in the United States, it is likely that many of those participating are relatively unaware of the actual complex historical events being celebrated and are instead enjoying the music, the festivities, the "crack"[3] of the day. For nationalists in the North of Ireland it is different, however, particularly for those trapped in isolated working class ghetto areas as the marchers crowd the streets on the boundaries of their area. For them the Twelfth is an annual reminder, like so many smaller daily reminders, that they were losers in the struggle over the establishment of the state. In that sense, nationalist attitudes to the Twelfth, as to other unionist symbols as diverse as the imposing devolved government building at Stormont or the national anthem played until recently in each cinema and theater at the end of the show, could be likened to those of native Americans to the United States bicentenary in 1977 or native Australians to their bicentenary in 1988: why should we celebrate their victory over us?

UNIONISM'S GOLDEN ERA

In the eighteen years from the establishment of the state to the beginning of World War II, the unionist alliance was at its most secure. This is not to say that there were not challenges to the alliance, in particular from working class unionists, and frequently on the basis of class demands. Thus, Protestants marched with Catholics in October 1932 demanding higher rates of pay and better conditions for those unemployed men working on Outdoor Relief schemes (Munck and Rolston 1987). Similarly, the working class Shankill area returned an independent unionist MP, Tommy Henderson, to the Northern parliament for the entire period from 1925 to 1953; Henderson's populist radicalism did not rest easy with the paternalistic conservatism of more mainstream unionism. Labour candidates had respectable electoral backing from unionist working class voters, especially in local government elections (Walker 1985). On the other hand, the challenge to established unionism also could come from the right, from working class unionists demanding that their leaders be more committed to opposing the evils of Republicanism and its socialist fellow travellers. Thus the "socialist upsurge" of October 1932 was followed shortly afterwards by the fierce sectarian trouble of July 1935. Although some commentators (Farrell 1980; Devlin 1981) put too much emphasis in explaining this change of heart on the unionist working class being mesmerised by the flag waving, drum beating, and high-pitched speech making of unionist leaders scared at incipient working class unity, it is clear that in 1935, as on other occasions in unionist history, the politicians were partly leading from behind.

Despite such strains, establishment of the Northern Ireland state placed the unionist alliance on a very secure base. The state provided the mechanisms that guaranteed continued unionist hegemony even in the face of the strongest opposition—the Special Powers Act, the B Specials, and the like. No longer was unionism an illegal force threatening independent action against the British parliament; it now had a devolved government established, recognized and underwritten by that parliament, albeit with certain notable gaps in relation to state power. Moreover, after the initial "teething troubles" of the state (including the deaths of almost 500 people within the first two years), there was no major internal threat to the state. Northern nationalists apparently had come to accept the fait accompli. The IRA in the North was a defeated force, not only as a result of state repression in the North, but also because of its isolation from the South. Unionism settled down contentedly into an apparent endless period of majority rule interrupted by the infrequent, sometimes noisy but ultimately ineffectual protests of representatives of the minority.

This cosiness and confidence were seen in the cultural sphere. The celebration of unionism and its state reached a crescendo during the summer, particularly around 12 July. Although the customs surrounding the celebration were by then well established, with the conviction that the state was here to stay, the cultural practices took on an aura of respectability surpassing even that which they had prior to the establishment of the state. Since at least the beginning of the century, unionist working class areas had seen the erection of street arches, the painting of curbstones, the hanging of bunting, the general improvements of houses and streets, the purchasing of Orange lodge banners, sashes, collarettes, and bowler hats, as well as the practizing of local bands preparing for the march on the Twelfth. But with the establishment of the state, these tasks nearly became a civic duty. Areas and streets within areas vied with each other for the most impressive arch; Brown Square in the Lower Shankill area managed to have a particularly ornate one each year, but there was always the risk of being upstaged.[4] Thus Earl Street in 1935 managed to capture the attention of the unionist media with its ingenious arch incorporating a model of the Siege of Derry. When the cord was cut at the unveiling by Captain Herbert Dixon MP, a model of the Williamite ship the Mountjoy was released and slid along the top of the arch toward the gates of the model city (see *Northern Whig*, 13 July 1935, p. 12). Arches were only part of an overall blitz of street decoration; for example, in 1939, Scott Street, off Sandy Row, had not only an arch at each end, but also strings of fairy lights for the entire length of the street (*Northern Whig*, 11 July 1939, p. 12). All of these decorations were paid for by local residents who also contributed to the equipment of a local band. Some of these bands were later known as "Kick the Pope" or "Blood and Thunder" bands, with their loud drumming, strutting, and baton twirling;[5] others were much more sedate. But the Orange lodges spared no expense, again competing with each other to have the best dressed marchers on the Twelfth, the finest banner and the best flute, brass, or accordion band. And part of the annual ritual was the painting and repainting of murals.

Like the other politico-cultural artifacts surrounding the Twelfth, exterior wall murals originated before the establishment of the Northern Ireland state. Their origins are later than the arches, banners, and the like, one reason being the absence of mass-produced paint. The availability of such paint, especially in industrial sites such as the shipyards, made the painting of large exterior wall murals feasible. Thus Loftus (1980a, p. 1) notes that Belfast's first unionist wall mural was painted in 1908 in the Beersbridge Road by John McLean, who was, not coincidentally, a shipyard worker. The subject of the mural was King Billy.

Loftus's research (1980a, pp. 1–2) has revealed that the range of themes covered in the murals was apparently wide.

> The ship named "Mountjoy" was shown breaking the boom maintained by the Jacobites against the Protestant defenders of Derry in 1688; Lord Roberts appeared flanked by two Boer War soldiers; the Ulster Division went over the top at the Battle of the Somme in action-packed detail; the

Angel of Mons hovered over the battlefield; the Titanic, built in Belfast's shipyards, went down with all the appeal of a disaster movie; King George V and Queen Mary were depicted at their coronation, their gilt chairs behind them receding in sharp perspective; the visit of the Prince of Wales to Northern Ireland was celebrated with a mural of him playing the great Lambeg drum, favourite instrument of Orangemen; and Victory was celebrated in 1945 with rising sun and fly past of aeroplanes.[6]

Unfortunately, photographic evidence of these early and interwar murals is sparse. The 1936 coronation mural mentioned above, painted on a gable wall in Little Ship Street, has

Little Ship Street. Coronation of King George V and Queen Mary, 1937. Photograph taken 1963; courtesy Belfast Central Library.

Fortingale Steet. Emblem of 36th Ulster Division which suffered massive losses at the Battle of the Somme, 1916. Artist: John McIlroy, pictured. (Source: Belfast Telegraph 10 July 1933, 12. Courtesy Belfast Telegraph.)

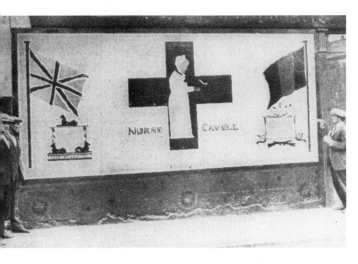

Primitive Street. Nurse Edith Cavell, executed in Belgium during World War I. Unnamed artists pictured. (Source: Belfast Telegraph 9 July 1929, 12. Courtesy: Belfast Telegraph.)

been captured for posterity (see *Sunday Times* color magazine, 23 March 1969), as has at least one depiction of the Battle of the Somme at Coolfin Street in 1935 (see *Weekly Belfast Telegraph,* 20 December 1935, p. 5). Although the Mountjoy mural mentioned by Loftus is long faded, the ship did appear frequently on arches; for example, on the arch at Cuba Street in 1939 (see *Belfast Telegraph,* 8 July 1939, p. 14). The emblem of the 36th Ulster Division, decimated at the Somme, was painted at Fortingale Street in 1933 by John McIlroy (see *Belfast Telegraph,* 10 July 1933, p. 12). The "Great War" also was commemorated in a 1929 mural in Primitive Street depicting Nurse Cavell, the British nurse executed by the Germans (see *Belfast Telegraph,* 9 July 1929, p. 12).

Yet the range of themes covered is more apparent than real—the most common theme was a depiction of King Billy. Although there were a number of historical incidents that could have been chosen as the subject of a mural—for example, the King landing at Carrickfergus, a theme chosen by Derry painter Bobby Jackson for one mural (a picture of which appears in Cooper and Sargent 1979, p. 39)—King Billy crossing the Boyne on a white horse was the most commonly depicted incident in the unionist repertoire.

The source for these "crossing the Boyne" murals was, as Loftus notes (1980a, p. 3), one of a series of postcards produced by a Belfast printing firm early in the century. Despite the common source, the range of quality of King Billy murals based on the one postcard was wide. Imagination was never allowed to run totally wild, although Bobby Jackson, whose Derry mural depicting the Mountjoy breaking the boom on the one hand and King Billy crossing the Boyne on the other is the oldest extant mural in Northern Ireland, claims he changed the color of William's horse from the probably more accurate black to a more aesthetic white because of a deathbed request by his mother (interview with Julian Watson 1982). Generally, the variety in the traditional King Billy murals derived more from the individual skill of the artist than from artistic flights of fancy.

Thus King Billy crossing the Boyne appeared in Tierney Street in 1936 as a relatively competently painted figure between ornate pillars and under an arch bearing a slogan common on

Tierney Street. King Billy crossing the Boyne. Artist: Fred Crone, pictured. (Source: Belfast News Letter *5 July 1939, 8. Courtesy:* Belfast News Letter.)

Shankill Road. King Billy crossing the Boyne. Artist: T. Henderson, 1930s. (Courtesy: Linenhall Library, Belfast.)

arches, "Cemented with Love" (see *Belfast Telegraph*, 11 July 1936, p. 12). The work was done by Howard Kelly with the assistance of Fred Crone. By 1939, the artists had added theaterlike curtains as a motif, as well as water dripping from the hoof of the horse emerging from a river that looks more like a lake (see *Belfast Newsletter*, 5 July 1939, p. 8). The ceremony of unveiling the repainted Tierney Street mural in 1939 was performed by the Independent unionist MP for the

area, Tommy Henderson (see *Belfast Telegraph*, 11 July 1939, p. 12). Henderson, a house painter by trade, painted a mural in the Shankill area in the 1930s; again, the curtain motif was used, as well as the device of containing the whole scene within an ornate frame, almost as if it were a portrait for which the King himself posed. The skill of the painter is apparent in this mural, but less grand murals also appeared. In 1933, E. Higginson tried valiantly in Roslyn Street, but, among other aspects, failed to do justice to the human features of King Billy (see *Belfast Telegraph*, 11 July 1933, p. 12). A 1937 mural in Templemore Street had a King Billy who looked uncomfortable on his squat, elongated horse (see *Belfast Newsletter*, 12 July 1937, p. 6).

Among the grandest attempts were two

murals that managed not only to maintain some semblance of perspective and proportionality, but, by introducing other figures, also managed to give more of a sense of action than is seen in all the previous murals of this period, with the exception of Jackson's already mentioned masterpiece. In Maria Street in 1934, King Billy is surrounded by buglers and other men on horseback; one can only guess at how much color was used in this impressive painting (see *Belfast Telegraph*, 12 July 1934, p. 12). In 1939 in Earl Lane, a mural obviously based on the same source as the Maria Place painting had added to it a frieze and the names of men killed during the sectarian riots in the area four years previously; "Their only crime was loyalty" noted the mural artist (see *Belfast Telegraph*, 7 July 1939, p. 20).

As Loftus (1980a, p. 4) notes, there have been "King Billys as elegant as an 18th century por-

Templemore Street. King Billy crossing the Boyne. (Source: Belfast Telegraph 11 July 1933, 12. Courtesy: Belfast Telegraph.)

Maria Place. King Billy crossing the Boyne. (Source: Belfast Telegraph. 12 July 1934, 12. Courtesy: Belfast Telegraph.)

Earl Lane. King Billy crossing the Boyne. (Source: Belfast Telegraph 7 July 1939, 20. Courtesy: Belfast Telegraph.)

trait or as boisterously vulgar as a piece of pop art." The reason for this is that the artists ranged from those who had previous painting experience to those who painted more from pleasure or political commitment than skill. At one end of the spectrum were men like George Wilgaus, who was not only a sign writer, banner painter and mural artist, but also had exhibited his own easel paintings. Then there was Bobby Jackson, who painted houses, coaches, banners, and drums. That Bobby's masterpiece in Derry exists to this day reveals another aspect of the loyalist tradition—the constant retouching, even redesigning of murals over time. Bobby Jackson helped his father to paint the Derry mural mentioned above in the mid-1920s. He repainted it through the years until his death in the 1980s. His son Bobby now is responsible for its upkeep, as well as carrying on another family tradition, that of building the annual 18-foot-high effigy of Lundy.[7]

Belfast's oldest extant loyalist mural, again of King Billy at the Boyne, also dates back to the 1920s. In 1969 it was redesigned for the first time in 39 years by George, William, and Gerald Dowie (see *Belfast Newsletter*, 12 July 1935, p. 2). More than twenty years later it still stands in Rockland Street after being retouched and redesigned in the preceding years, each time reflecting the skill of the artists involved. It is a relatively simple portrait style painting of King Billy (the most common variant) rather than an action-packed mural.

Artists had a high status in the community. They were permitted, even encouraged, by community and state to use their skills, however rudimentary, to celebrate William's victory, and the unionist state eventually built on that victory. The unveiling of the mural each July thus became a state occasion, a microcosm of the unionist alliance at its most secure. The unveiling was performed by an MP or judge, an army officer or minister, a landowner or businessman. Those at the pinnacle of the unionist alliance said something profound about the importance of preserving the Protestant inheritance left for them by King William and about never weakening in the face of Ulster's enemies. The local crowd, proud of their mural, listened attentively to this timeless, quasi-religious message and the whole event had a ritualistic importance. In a real sense, the actual words spoken did not matter, nor did the quality of the painting. What was important was that they were there commemorating the event. Like the unionist state, the alliance and its rituals were here to stay.

Given the civic importance of the annual event, no one dared interfere with the mural artist or his product. As Loftus (1980a, p. 4) says of James Hume, shipyard worker and mural painter, he chose whichever gable wall he wanted, even if it were on the side of the local police station.

THE POSTWAR YEARS: CHANGE AND DECAY

World War I, and particularly the fate of the Ulster Division at the Battle of the Somme, did much to strengthen unionist identity and thereby the unionist alliance. A similar process might have been expected after World War II, but this was not to be. The inauguration of the welfare state counteracted any tendencies to enhance unionist collective identity; the welfare state became an element in fracturing the unionist alliance.

Devolution meant a level of independence, but a very relative one. Northern Ireland as a state had to adhere, for the most part, to British legislative and policy changes. This became known as the "step by step" policy and ensured that, despite its own elements of unique legislation (such as the Special Powers Act) and its derogation from certain aspects of British legislation (especially relating to marriage and sexuality), Northern Ireland law followed British law. The wave of enthusiasm for social reform that swept over Britain in the aftermath of World War II effected important political changes in Northern Ireland. But there was less of a clearly articulated popular outcry for social reform in Northern Ireland. Moreover, Northern Ireland MPs at Westminster voted against the very legislation they administered later. There were even moves to demand Dominion status to avoid having to implement the reforms. Northern Ireland became part of the welfare state against its will.

The arrival of the welfare state began a process that later helped splinter unionism. For a start, its universalist principles led to benefits for nationalists that they would not have gained under a Northern Ireland legislature. Thus, the provision in the late 1940s of free education at grammar school and university on the basis of merit meant the arrival, twenty years later, of a new class of articulate, educated nationalists impatient for social change.

But the welfare state had also introduced a series of specific contradictions into the heart of unionism itself. Not only was there the paradox of an ultra-conservative government in charge of enacting social democratic policies, but the ideology of progress and modernization also grated with the almost feudal traditionalism of unionism. In short, the alliance began to come under strain. Socialism became relatively popular in unionist working class circles; by 1962 there were seven Northern Ireland Labour Party MPs at Stormont (out of a total of 52), the highest number ever. The trade unions began to demand the recognition afforded them in normal social democratic states; by 1964 that demand was belatedly conceded with the recognition of the Northern Ireland Committee of the Irish Congress of Trade Unions by the Stormont government. Socialists, trade unionists, liberal academics, churchmen, and others began to make demands relating to the obvious decline of the traditional industries on which the North's economy was based, shipbuilding and linen. Their solution, cogently argued by Isles and Cuthbert (1957), two Queen's University economists, was to create a package of incentives to entice foreign capital to invest in and thus revive the teetering economy. This solution met support from within Unionist Party circles from more enlightened and liberal members (in economic terms at least) whose feet were not firmly placed in traditional industry. Those unionists whose existence depended on the survival of local industry were less prone to economic liberalism, less supportive of enticements to foreign industry. The antagonism between these two fractions of the unionist bourgeoisie was apparent as early as 1946, as O'Dowd (1980, p. 37)

notes when quoting local industrialist Walter Smiles's derisory rejection of foreign industry in favor of industry "deeply rooted in the soil of Ulster." By the late 1960s, the antagonism was fully out in the open.

At the ideological level, this antagonism was expressed in debates about tradition versus progress, sectarianism versus non-sectarianism, state intervention versus laissez faire, and so on. One of the most contentious questions was whether capable middle-class Catholics should continue to be blocked economically and politically. Ultimately it was only a matter of time before reforms allowed space for the emergence of some Catholic unionists and only a short time more before liberal Protestant unionists recognized the need to incorporate them in some way. The Unionist Party was never able to open its doors to Catholic unionists, but new parties eventually emerged to allow them space (the Alliance Party, for example). Catholics in the Unionist Party—to traditionalists this was probably the ultimate treasonable act. It underlined the fact that the old ideological certainties, although not yet dealt a mortal blow, were under severe attack. The uncertainty and questioning of traditional identity became apparent at the level of cultural practices, not so much in the actual content of those practices as in the extent of their overall decline.

During World War II, the Twelfth marches were suspended; the contemporary war effort took precedence over the celebration of a past war. But a *Belfast Telegraph* (12 July 1941) reporter, commenting on the absence of the traditional festivities in 1941, pointed out a least one strand of continuity—the loyalty of the unionist working class.

> Today was the quietest Twelfth in Ulster's history. Instead of putting on their sashes and collarettes and setting out for the assembly point for the march to the "Field," Belfast Orangemen put on their dungarees and working clothes and went to work as usual in shipyard and factory. . . . There were a few striking arches in the Shankill and other districts noted for their loyalty, but otherwise this colourful note so closely associated with the glorious Twelfth was conspicuous by its absence. . . . "No, this hasn't the slightest resemblance to the Twelfth," said one Orangeman to a "Telegraph" reporter, "but never fear, we'll make

up for it when Hitler's walloped. The next Twelfth we have will put all the other Twelfths in the shade."

It did. The "biggest Twelfth ever" was seen in 1946, according to the *Northern Whig* (13 July 1946), which also commented on massive recruitment to the Orange Order. A loyalist revival did seem to be afoot in other areas as well. Like the *Belfast Telegraph*, the *Belfast Newsletter* (12 July 1940) noted that, even in the absence of the traditional march, "the spirit of the Twelfth lives on," and showed two pictures of arches to underline the point. When the war ended this newspaper, like the others mentioned, returned to its custom of presenting pictures of such arches in its editions around the Twelfth. The *Belfast Newsletter* (4 July 1951) also noted houses on the Crumlin Road freshly painted for the holiday. On 10 July 1959 it carried a photograph and article about an arch across the main Shankill Road, "believed to be the first arch erected on the Shankill Road since 1901." The *Northern Whig* (13 July 1957) noted another first; Enniskillen Loyal Orange Lodge number 387 in Toronto carried a banner on the Twelfth march that pictured Queen Elizabeth II, "the first ever to have a picture of a living monarch on it."

By the end of the 1950s and start of the 1960s, a number of newspaper articles began to hint at rumblings of changed times. In 1963, for example, the *Belfast Newsletter* (9 July 1963) noted that the number of Orange arches continued to increase. It quoted Walter Williams, Secretary of the Grand Lodge of Ireland:

> Since the war we have had at least one new one every Twelfth. Materials are so plentiful now and residents in the streets don't mind so much parting with a bob or two.

On the other hand, the same article declared quite definitively that "the practice of painting King William murals on gables at the corners of Belfast streets is slowly dying." The reporter located only one mural in good condition, a King Billy at Silvergrove Street. The painter of this mural, Harold Gibson, a boilerman at the nearby Ormeau Baths, complained that

> "the trouble is that people don't have them repainted until they are almost faded away. I first painted the big one in Silvergrove Street in 1938, but it was not until 1960 that I did it again."

Silvergrove Street. King Billy crossing the Boyne. Artist: Harold Gibson. (Source: Belfast News Letter *9 July 1963, 7. Courtesy:* Belfast News Letter.*)*

Both Gibson and the reporter were at a loss to explain why the traditional art form was dying out, the reporter adding that "at £10 a mural it is not really an expensive decoration."

In an article in the *Sunday Press* the following year (26 January 1964), Belfast playwright and actor Joseph Tomelty also was unable to ascertain the reason for the "dying art of gable painting." He noted that the King Billy at Rockland Street rode a horse that only a few years previously had been whiter than white but was now "greyer than grey." And he also discovered an incredibly amateur mural of King Billy at Northumberland Street (pictured in the article) that was not only "disappointing" but also "surrealistically shocking."

Despite the optimism of the Secretary of the Orange Order noted above, it would appear that the cultural decline also affected the annual erection of arches. Writing in the *Belfast Telegraph* (11 July 1959), Barry White named eleven streets that had arches that year (five of which were pictured). However, there also were twenty streets mentioned that no longer had their traditional arches. In addition, he noted, one of the current arches, at Memel Street, would not be erected in the coming year, thus breaking a more than seventy-year tradition in that street. The article ventures three explanations. Firstly, quoting one man, White writes, "everyone enjoys the fun of an arch, but they're not willing to do the donkey work." Secondly,

> Increased costs are another reason for the decline. An arch which might have cost much less than £100 before the war costs fully £200–300 today for materials alone.

An old man quoted ventured a third, less specific reason: "It's a sign of the time. People have too much else to think about these days."

Similarly, the Lambeg drum making business was waning. A *Belfast Newsletter* reporter (2 July 1966) quoted Thomas Johnston, whose family had been making drums since 1890, as saying that "Lambegs may soon be a noisy memory of the past." The reasons given were that there were fewer bands than 25 years before, that many of them no longer wanted Lambegs because they "slow up a procession," and that the bands that did want them could buy them from English firms. "It is all a question of economics," concluded Johnston.

The traditional cultural practices were not totally dead, however. Banner painting, for example, was enough in demand to allow Frank Hargy of Portrush to earn his living solely as a painter of Orange banners in 1958, the first member of his family in three generations of the tradition to be able to do so (see *Belfast Telegraph*, 4 July 1958). At the same time, there were clear signs of cultural decay in the postwar period, variously explained in terms of increasing cost, lack of interest, selfishness, consumerism, and something as nebulous as "the modern age." But, considering that cultural practices and artifacts somehow reveal underlying ideology, it can be said that the beginnings of unionist uncertainty were reflected in the decline of traditional cultural expression. Thus the lack of

murals, arches, and Lambeg drums was a harbinger of impending explosive rifts in the unionist state. The unionist alliance was about to embark on its period of least unity. The golden age of unionist culture was on the wane, perhaps never to return.

Commentators such as Joseph Tomelty realized that the passing of the golden age was visible on unionist walls. There were fewer murals painted, and fewer still of reputable quality. The tradition of retouching the murals for the annual

Earl Street. King Billy crossing the Boyne; Ian Paisley addresses the crowd at mural's dedication. (Source: Belfast Telegraph 9 July 1965, 2. Courtesy: Belfast Telegraph.)

Eighth Street. King Billy crossing the Boyne. Unnamed artists pictured. (Source: Belfast Telegraph *8 July 1965, 3. Courtesy:* Belfast Telegraph.*)*

Hudson Place. King Billy crossing the Boyne. Unnamed artists pictured. (Source: Belfast News Letter *12 July 1967, 5. Courtesy:* Belfast News Letter.*)*

celebrations also declined, but there were exceptions. Adequately executed life-size portraits of Queen Elizabeth and Prince Philip were hung on an exterior wall in Malvern Street in 1955 (see *Belfast Newsletter,* 9 July 1955, p. 8) and Earl Street's King Billy mural mentioned earlier, dating back to the 1930s, continued to be retouched in the 1960s and in 1965 was unveiled by a preacher of rising popularity, Ian Paisley (see *Belfast Telegraph,* 9 July 1965, p. 2).[8] But these were exceptions. Eighth Street in 1965 (see *Belfast Telegraph,* 8 July 1965, p. 3) and Hudson Place in 1967 (see *Belfast Newsletter,* 12 July 1967, p. 5) are more typical: amateur King Billys were no longer painted by adults with a long-term commitment to the ritual but by youths and children. Loyalist mural painting was at a nadir compared to the heyday of John McLean and Bobby Jackson.

Johnston (1970, p. 206), echoing points made by other commentators quoted above, summed up the situation.

. . . recent years have witnessed a decline in wall paintings and the competitive spirit in arch design between neighbouring loyalist streets. As local authorities demolish sub-standard dwellings to make way for the new, and tenants move out to the suburbs, the tradition of writing and illustrating Ireland's tragic history in the street wanes. . . .

Even the rhetoric had changed. Sectarian utterances had become less fashionable. Therefore when in the run up to the Twelfth in 1965 someone painted "Ulster is British," "No Surrender," "Kick the Pope," and "Remember 1690" on a bridge in Lisburn, the Minister of Home Affairs himself, R. W. B. McConnell, condemned the action.

No section of the community should put up slogans which give offence to other people. I hope slogans which give offence will die out in this country. (*Belfast Telegraph*, 3 July 1965)

THE ARRIVAL OF THE "TROUBLES"

McConnell's wish, whether genuine or merely rhetorical, was not to be fulfilled. By 1965 the foundations of major dissent against unionist rule were already being laid. Within a few years a full-fledged civil rights movement emerged. The unionist alliance, already showing signs of a split between liberals and hardliners, was dealt another major blow, reacting to the civil rights demands with promises of reform on the one hand and the reality of repression on the other. It was a short step from that to the reemergence of open and violent conflict, by which point offensive slogans were the least that people had to worry about.

The origins of civil rights are not only in the traditional rejection of the Northern state and its institutions, but also in the emergence of one important effect of the postwar welfare state, namely, an educated and articulate Catholic middle class. With horizons wider than those of traditional conservative nationalists, and especially influenced by the example of civil rights struggles in the United States, Catholic middle-class students joined with some trade unionists, socialists, communists, nationalists, and republicans to demand reforms in housing allocation, the disbandment of the B Specials, the repeal of the Special Powers Act, the end of gerrymandering in local government, and above all, "one man, one vote."

It could be argued that the immediate concession of those demands would have placated many civil rights activists. The civil rights movement, with its core consisting of people who had grown up experiencing all the postwar benefits of the union with Britain, was much more oriented toward reforms *within* the Northern Ireland state than the abolition of the Northern Ireland state itself. True, there were some republicans and communists involved who saw democratic reform as a step toward a united Ireland, and other more traditional republicans who became involved in civil rights agitation in the absence of any military campaign. For the most part, however, unionism's most self-protective response would have been to concede as many civil rights demands as possible as quickly as possible.

But the civil rights movement confronted a unionist bloc already splitting into hardline and liberal factions. As early as 1965, the UVF formed in opposition to the supposedly treacherous appeasement of nationalists being shown by the liberal Prime Minister Terence O'Neill. In 1966 the UVF committed its first sectarian murder; three members, including Gusty Spence, the founder of the organization, were sentenced to life imprisonment. Liberal unionists thus had to attempt to steer a course between the civil rights demands and the determination of more strident loyalists not to concede to any such demands.

For those in the loyalist camp, the state was clearly founded on the basis of containing and controlling the nationalist minority. Any attempt to weaken the mechanisms of containment and control thus were not only treasonable but also potentially suicidal in political terms. Therefore the civil rights movement met with open repression, and out of that backlash the IRA eventually reemerged in its traditional role as a defender of nationalist areas.

Before the birth and growth of the Provisional IRA (Irish Republican Army), however, another factor appeared that was more devastating to unionist self-identity and confidence. The British government intervened, first by sending in soldiers to protect nationalists from the RUC (Royal Ulster Constabulary) and B Specials, and second by beginning to institute reforms that liberal unionism had been unable and loyalism unwilling to concede previously. In 1970 the British instituted almost every civil rights demand, including the disbandment of the B Specials and the (temporary) disarming of the RUC. In 1972 they prorogued Stormont itself; and in 1973–1974, they instituted a devolved Assembly with two very nonunionist elements: executive power-sharing between nationalists and unionists, and a proposed Council of Ireland. Liberal unionists found a niche in going along with the British reforms and were rewarded with the task of instituting them. But loyalists were caught in a dilemma they had not experienced for sixty years; that is, opposing Britain in the name of being British. Old notions of conditional loyalty arose, and the dilemma was solved partially by emphasizing that loyalist allegiance was to the British monarch rather than the British government. Hence there was the apparently paradoxical notion of MP Robert Bradford that "the time might come when Ulstermen would have to become Queen's rebels in order to remain citizens of any kind" (August 1975, cited in Miller 1978); or of Billy Hull, founder of the Loyalist Association of Workers: "We are British to the core, but we won't hesitate to take on even the British if they attempt to sell our country down the river" (cited in Janke 1983, p. 93).

Also helpful as a way out of ideological confusion was the notion of Ian Paisley and his Free Presbyterian Church that unionists in Northern Ireland were the last remaining "true Brits," retaining the old ideals of Protestantism long after the British people and government had succumbed to ecumenism, sodomy, abortion, and "the continental Sunday." Thus, according to the Free Presbyterian paper *Protestant Telegraph* (14 December 1968), in Britain,

> nearly all the methods of propaganda are now fairly controlled by the Roman Catholic church—cinema, television, newspapers and magazines. Their representatives were carefully selected while posts were being prepared in political parties, trade unions, universities and Protestant churches. Northern Ireland being the last bulwark of Protestantism in Europe, if not the world, was singled out for special attention.

But such subtleties of rationalization did little to conceal the underlying shock to unionist identity. As loyalism grew in strength, many of the grand old institutions of unionism were seen as effete and ineffectual, full only of timid members of the "fur-coated brigade." Institutions such as the Orange Order went into decline in the 1970s to be replaced by mass organizations such as the UDA (Ulster Defence Association). But there was a major difference between the two types of organization. The Orange Order represented the unionist alliance in its purest form—all classes of unionism marching together with the factory owners and landowners in the lead. The UDA as a mass organization was overwhelmingly working class, with a leadership that was at most petit bourgeois. Its efforts were directed mostly against the traditional unionist leaders. If those leaders joined with them in a common alliance—such as during the UWC (Ulster Workers' Council) strike in 1974 that brought down the power-sharing executive—it was often ad hoc and full of mutual suspicion. At various points throughout the 1970s, even the most staunch loyalist politicians found themselves leading from behind.

The UDA marched, frequently in numbers rivaling what the Orange Order in its heyday could have mustered. But these were not the ritualistic Twelfth marches, complete with banners, horse-drawn carriages, and bowler hats. The loyalist marches of the 1970s were much less ritualistic and much more situational and openly political. Loyalist Association of Workers members marched in force to demand the internment of republicans in 1971. Vanguard members marched and paraded in 1972 in a style reminiscent of Nurnburg in the thirties. Tens of thousands UDA men marched in the early and mid-1970s, masked and wearing combat gear.

Despite the ability of such populist organizations to put so many marching men on the streets, the popularity of 12 July marches declined. As it had done in the previous decade, the *Belfast Newsletter* continued to blame the rising cost of staging the traditional parades. For example, in 1974 *Belfast Newsletter* (12 July 1974) reporter Alan Whitsitt asked: ". . . how long can the Orange Order continue to stage the Twelfth on such a grand scale, or indeed can the brethren afford to meet its cost?" But such solely financial considerations miss the fundamental point that cultural decline accurately measured ideological confusion. Why celebrate a ritual when the old sureties are under fire? Why parade the traditional symbols when the overarching symbol, the devolved parliament at Stormont itself, has been prorogued by the British?

Thus, it was not merely that the Orange Order's march on the Twelfth was less popular at a time when other organizations were able to arrange monster rallies and marches. The declin-

Crumlin Road. King Billy crossing the Boyne.

Larne, Country Antrim, 1978. Loyalist symbols, including Jacob's Ladder, the "Mountjoy" ship, and King Billy crossing the Boyne.

ing tradition of erecting arches declined further in the 1970s. Few of the streets that had erected arches for generations continued to do so. This occurred in part because many of the streets ceased to exist after massive redevelopment in the 1970s.[9] But cultural decline helped ensure that no new arches appeared in the new streets. Sandy Row kept its expensive arch, as did some smaller towns and villages. But they increasingly became exceptions that proved the rule.

As in other periods, mural painting became an accurate barometer of the political atmosphere.

With a few exceptions, such as the Rockland Street King Billy mentioned earlier, the old murals were not retouched. Many walls showed only the ghostly shadows of previously bright murals. But the cultural practice did not die totally. Instead, there was an almost frantic scrambling for new images to fit the times. Although there were a number of new murals, there were few depicting King Billy. One well painted and very traditional one appeared in the center of Coleraine, complete with the Union Jack, the Ulster flag, and the flag of St. Andrew. A slightly less competent King Billy, but more original in its framing of the central character, was painted on the Crumlin Road in Belfast; there were flags, as well as a crown, Orange lilies, and an Ulster shield. Finally, in Larne a figure of King Billy was one of many symbols on a long low wall, including a Union Jack, a ladder, a goat, a cock, and a ship. Many of these symbols were themselves traditional Orange ones with strong biblical connections and had appeared frequently in arches throughout the years. But what is interesting about them in this context is that they represent a trend that grew in significance in the 1970s, namely, the displacement of historico-mythical representations and the appearance of inanimate emblems as the centerpiece of murals. Prominent among these emblems were flags, particularly the Union Jack and Ulster Flag, frequently given equal prominence. The Red Hand of Ulster, a traditional loyalist symbol, also figured in murals, as it also did in the emblem of the largest loyalist organization, the UDA. In at least one case, a Red Hand nearly two meters in height was the centerpiece of a crude mural in the Village area of South Belfast. This area had housed one of the loyalist gangs active in the mid-1970s in the killing of nationalist civilians. Hence, apart from acknowledging the two loyalist paramilitary groups, the UVF and the UDA, the mural celebrates the achievements of the VAS—the Village Assassination Squad.

Loyalist mural painters had a problem finding new symbols to serve as the rallying point for a confused unionism. In reality, the relationship between cause and effect operated in the opposite direction. The confusion of unionism presented mural painters—no less than other unionists—with the problem of finding a new

Lecale Street, 1982. Red Hand of Ulster and VAS (Village Assassination Squad).

Rathcoole. Red Devils; "Who Dares Wins."

consensus to replace the old. The new symbols could not precede the new consensus. A valiant attempt was made by youths in the Rathcoole estate north of Belfast. Similar to unionist youths in other areas, they organized into Tartan gangs (so named because some tartan article of clothing was an essential part of their uniform) and symbolized more clearly than anything else the ruptures in the traditional alliance. Having few connections to the old traditions and organizations, and owing their allegiance more to the new paramilitary organizations, the Tartan gangs were both a new loyalist symbol and the creators of new symbols. Thus in Rathcoole, they plundered widely to find inspiration for their murals. In one, the Red Devils of Manchester United Football Club coexist with the slogan of

the SAS (Special Air Services), "Who Dares Wins," while the centerpiece is a slogan dormant in loyalist circles for forty years, "KAI"—"Kill All Irish."[10] Nearby was the ultimate in witty originality; alongside the traditional slogan "FTP" ("Fuck the Pope") is a representation of Pope John Paul II waving the scarf of a supporter of Linfield, Belfast's loyalist soccer team. For the young Tartans, one must conclude that the degradation envisaged in the picture would be greater for the Pope than that urged in the adjoining slogan.

Despite the wittiness of these murals, however, they display cultural confusion rather than a newly forged cultural certainty. In a similar vein, one of the most ornate loyalist murals of the 1970s makes a pictorial statement that is more grand than the political content treated by the mural. For loyalist paramilitaries, the notion that they should be imprisoned for loyalty was the ultimate insult. Politically as well as psychologically, it was difficult to accept being jailed by British authorities for actions performed to keep Ulster British. Tim Pat Coogan captured this sense of political shock well when writing about a personal visit to the loyalist compound in Long Kesh.

One is a "loyalist" but he is not quite as certain as he was that the Crown he is loyal to is that concerned with him. Certainly if he is in prison for an excess of loyalism, i.e. shooting or otherwise putting down the treacherous Fenian Catholic, he

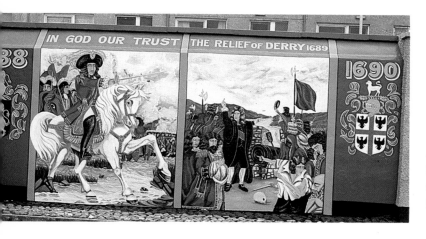

Fountain, Derry, 1920s. (Left) King Billy crossing the Boyne, 1690 and (right) the "Mountjoy" breaking the Siege of Derry, 1689. Artist: Bobby Jackson. (Photograph taken in 1983.)

Coleraine, County Derry. King Billy crossing the Boyne.

Donegall Road. King Billy crossing the Boyne. (Photograph taken 1984.)

North Street, Ballymena. King Billy crossing the Boyne.

Lindsay Street, 1984. King Billy crossing the Boyne; dying Jacobite soldier on river bank.

Lindsay Street. Flags, shields, and crown; "Remember the loyalist prisoners."

Percy Place, 1984. Street prepared for 12 July: arch, flags, shields, and painted kerbstones.

Crumlin Road, 1987. Ulster Volunteer Force in action.

Lindsay Street, 1983. Memorial to Rev. Robert Bradford, MP, killed by IRA.

Ainsworth Avenue, 1984. Armed loyalist sentry nationalist area.

Meekon Street, 1988. (Top) Red Hand of Ulster "dances" on Irish tricolor in protest at Anglo-Irish Agreement; (bottom) commemoration of the 75th anniversary of formation of the Ulster Volunteer Force.

Dervock, County Antrim. Ulster Division in action at Battle of the Somme, 1916.

Albertbridge Road, 1988. Commemoration of Battle of the Somme, 1916; "But Never Heart Forget."

Craven Street, 1988. (Left) continuity of loyalist military activity; Ulster Volunteer Force in World War I and (right) in Long Kesh prison.

Shankill Road, 1988. "Ulster" portrayed as woman calling men to arms, 1914.

Hogarth Street, 1988. Young loyalist painters at work on mural of King Billy crossing the Boyne.

Shankill Road, 1988. Apprentice Boys shutting the gates of Derry, 1689.

Disraeli Street, 1977. Local youngsters. (Artists: Ray McCullough and Ernie Francis.)

Torrens Avenue, 1978. Circus scene. (Artists: Joan Clarke and Virginia Doloughan.)

Ainsworth Avenue, 1978. Welders. (Artists: John Carson and Maureen Davis.)

oden Street, 1978. Skateboarder. (Artists: John ooney and Cathal Caldwell.)

Rossville Street, 1981. Busts of ten republicans who died on hunger strike.

Upper Meadow Street, 1988. Men playing hurling and Gaelic football.

Whiterock Road, 1981. Angel, dying hunger stri and IRA volunteer; "Blessed are those who hunger justice."

Rockmore Road, 1981. Defiant blanketman; "Break Thatcher's Back." (Courtesy: Dave and Marilyn Hyndman.)

Rockmount Street, 1981. Dying hunger striker and Blessed Virgin; "Blessed are those who hunger for justice".

Brompton Park, 1981. Firing party and coffin draped in tricolor; "The Final Salute."

Andersonstown Road, 1981. Armed republican volunteer in front of tricolor and flag of Na Fianna Eireann; "Venceremos."

Rockville Street, 1981. IRA unit in action.

Twinbrook, 1982. Triumphant blanketman and continuity of republican struggle.

Beechmount Avenue, 1983. Election mural; "For a New Ireland."

Andersonstown Road, 1981. Phoenix breaking H of H Blocks, words of popular song, "A Nation Once Again."

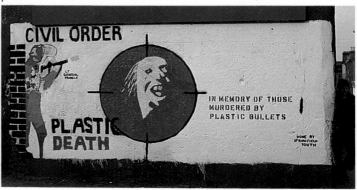

Sevastapol Street, 1982. Advertisement for An Phoblacht/Republican News.

Linden Street, 1981. "In memory of those murdered by plastic bullets."

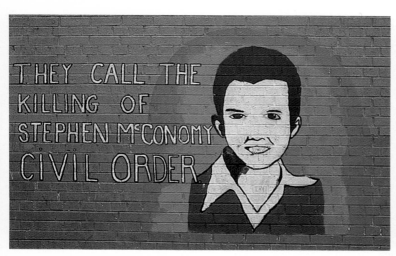

Rossville Street, Derry, 1982. Memorial to Stephen McConomy, aged 11, killed by plastic bullet.

Beechmount Avenue, 1984. IRA unit in action.

Springhill Avenue, 1987. IRA volunteers brandishing weapons.

Rathcoole. The Pope waving a loyalist scarf.

finds his sense of identity under a severe strain as he looks out through barbed wire at British uniforms keeping him there. In the old days of the Tory Unionist alliance some of his forebears got jobs and houses through similar activities. I found the UVF compounds particularly sad and ironic in this context. Their huts are all called after World War I battlefields in which their forefathers distinguished themselves—"Ypres," "Paschandaele," "Thiepval Wood" and all the other brave wasteful futilities. Today's UVF are one of the withdrawal pangs of empire. (Coogan 1980, pp. 203–204)

For the unionist community outside the prisons, there was frequently a sense of embarrassment in relation to loyalist prisoners. Thus a mural in Lindsay Street urging people to "Remember the loyalist prisoners" is more of an accusation than a celebration. Its grand statement in flags, Red Hands, the crown, and the motto of the UDA, "quis separabit—who shall separate," is at odds with the often minimal support given on the loyalist side to campaigns around prison issues. Certainly nothing as ornate, colorful, and confident as the flag created by UDA prisoners in Long Kesh in 1974 ever adorned loyalist walls. (See Hayes-McCoy 1979, p. 233, for a photograph of the flag; the flag itself, painted on a sheet, is kept in the Ulster Museum.) This mural, depicts the reality of an intact and tight military command structure among political prisoners, with "loyalist prisoners of war" shown bearing their flags and standing at

attention in front of the huts and watch towers of Long Kesh.

Similar problems of meaning existed in relation to the actions for which the loyalists were imprisoned originally. Republicans could easily present their struggle as one against a mighty imperialist aggressor and draw on numerous images, both local and foreign, to depict that representation. Loyalists had a problem. Where exactly was the enemy when the enemy was everyone other than the staunchest loyalists? Even if republicanism was judged the main enemy, how was one to use guerrilla tactics against these able guerrillas? Frequently, the loyalist answer was to assassinate ordinary nationalists, hoping to terrorize the community into withdrawing support for republican activists. Between January 1971 and June 1984,

> loyalist paramilitary victims are nearly all (562 out of a total of 619) civilians. Loyalist paramilitaries have killed more civilians than nationalist paramilitaries (562 versus 484). (Roche 1984, p. 6)

This was not the kind of heroic struggle depicted easily in symbolic form. There was a major difference between "guerrilla action against an armed foreign aggressor" and the slaughter of an individual heading to work or returning from a night out drinking. Although republican paramilitaries later became involved in random assassinations of civilians, they still could fall back on other representation. Loyalists lacked this back-up. Therefore, despite the level of loyalist

The Fountain, Derry. Portrait of a Red Hand Commando and emblem of the Ulster Defence Association.

paramilitary activity and the strength of paramilitary organizations in the 1970s, there was little attempt to portray loyalist armed struggle in murals.

One notable exception was in the Fountain area of Derry where the painted bust of a man in a uniform consisting of a black jacket, beret, and sunglasses was acknowledged in the caption as a member of the Red Hand Commandos, an offshoot of the UVF and an organization responsible for a number of sectarian assassinations. Although anonymous, the portrait was modeled loosely on a photograph of Gusty Spence, the then legendary figurehead of militant loyalism.

INTO THE EIGHTIES

The 1981 republican hunger strike, as we shall see in chapter 3, proved a turning point for the republican movement both in terms of political development and the emergence of mural painting. It did not, however, have a similar effect on unionism. To take one example: there were no loyalist murals produced to counter the tremendous propaganda boost gained by republicans through the hunger strike. At most there were quasi-murals, carefully painted slogans with messages of open hostility. "The time is now for Sands to die," said one Sandy Row slogan of leading hunger striker Bobby Sands. Further down Sandy Row in a weird juxtaposition of images was the message "Let Bobby Sands die" on the wall of a bakery on which there also is a cigarette advertisement referring to Britain and Ireland as "black on the map." The *i* of "die" was in the form of a cross. In nearby Donegall Pass was the crudest of messages, mimicking the advertising slogan for Haig whiskey: "Don't be vague, starve a taig" (*taig* being a slang word for Catholic).

The republican hunger strike did not galvanize the disparate sections of unionism (albeit in opposition) in the same way as it did nationalism. It could be argued that nothing came close to doing precisely that since the onset of the troubles, with the exception of the brief burst of unity in opposition to the power-sharing executive of 1974. The root of the problem of unionist unity was still the dilemma over identity. Politically, various unionists in the 1970s and 1980s have favored solutions as diverse as complete integration with Britain; the restoration of devolved government at Stormont, with or without power sharing; and independence for Northern Ireland, negotiated or declared unilaterally. In the midst of such political diffusion, it should

Sandy Row, 1981. "Let Bobby Sands Die."

not be surprising that there was a search to redeem old symbols or find new ones to match the times.

Part of this search involved unionism digging for its roots. Thus unionism was working with the distinct impression that it was culturally impoverished in relation to nationalism. Nationalism could trace its roots back not just to the Easter Rising of 1916, but to the "Celtic mists" of the sixth century and before. The idea that the present was rooted in the distant Celtic past inspired figures as different as W. B. Yeats the poet and James Connolly the socialist and revolutionary (in his *Labour in Irish History,* first published in 1910). Whether this history was mythologized or to what extent is not the point; the point is that it was regarded as the sole intellectual property of nationalists.

In previous generations it had been sufficient for unionists to recount the glories of the Somme or the Boyne, the two rivers whose influence has been the source of much twentieth-century unionist ideology and identity. But increasingly during the postrepublican hunger strike period, this was judged to be insufficient. "For far too many the term 'Ulster culture' signifies nothing more than Orangemen parading on the 12th July." This is the opinion of the Young Unionist Council, a section of the Official Unionist Party, the main unionist party. They argued further that

> for too long we have been content to neglect our culture while gaelic nationalism has made every effort and used every opportunity to propound Irish culture. (1986, p. 1)

The time had come to redeem some of that history for unionism.

In their search for roots, the Young Unionists had had the path prepared for them by a book originally published twelve years previously. Adamson (1974) meticulously recreated the history of the Cruthin (or Picts), the pre-Milesian inhabitants of the northern part of Ireland. The Cruthin were overrun by the expansion of the Celts. Some became vassals of the powerful O'Neill clan that held power in Ulster until the Elizabethan plantations; others were forced to flee to Scotland. The political message of the Cruthin story to contemporary loyalists was therefore threefold. First, it was a counterclaim to nationalist mythology: "we were here first." Second, heroes and achievements claimed by nationalists were judged to have been "hijacked" by them. For example, Cuchulain, the great warrior who defended Ulster against the invading Celts, was a Cruthin. The influential sixth-cen-

tury monastery at Bangor, County Down, was Cruthin, not Celt (Adamson 1979). Third, and perhaps most important, the planters who went from Scotland to Ulster in the seventeenth century could be said to have been merely returning home, "claiming their birthright," as the Young Unionists put it (1986, p. 2). Adamson, writing under his pen name Sam Sloan in the UDA's magazine *Ulster* (October 1978), sums it up.

> You are the children of the Cruthin, the sons and daughters of the Picts. This is OUR land, YOUR culture, YOUR heritage—you are indeed the people. You are older than the Gaels, older than the Welsh, older even than the English.

Thus Adamson's more emotional statements found sympathy with the UDA, more accurately its commander, Andy Tyrie. But the revisionism inherent in the Cruthin thesis did not please all sections of unionism, whether within or outside the UDA. Gusty Spence of the UVF and Sammy Smyth of the UDA were learning some Irish, but not every unionist could get over the gut feeling that the Irish language was part of the politics of Ulster's traditional enemies.[11] In addition, with its unstated but no less real assumption of two nations existing in Ireland, the Cruthin argument probably found most favor with unionists who supported an independent Northern Ireland. Its claims of Ulster's totally separate identity were less acceptable to unionists who hoped for a devolved parliament within the United Kingdom or complete integration with Britain. Outside of certain sections of the UDA, the argument found little support for a long time. Its belated and apparently brief adoption by the Young Unionists (but interestingly not by the Official Unionist Party as a whole) owed more to the unionist response to the 1985 Anglo-Irish Agreement than to the overwhelming persuasion of the argument itself.

Adamson's thesis went further. To fill the gap between the sixth century and the present, he revised other aspects of what had been seen as solely nationalist history. Thus United Irishmen such as the "noble" Henry Joy McCracken (Adamson 1974, p. 87) and "the brave idealist" Theobald Wolfe Tone were Cruthin, not Celts, (were "ours," not "theirs"). For some unionists, this revisionism went too far. Even the Young Unionists (1986, p. 3), paraphrasing Adamson, felt it necessary to dilute the political message (1976, p. 3):

> "we may not agree with the stance of our Presbyterian United Irishmen in 1798, but we should never forget . . . that their stand was essentially one against injustice and misrule."

Although the Cruthin thesis was interesting and original, it did not become the means whereby a relatively disjointed unionism could be reunited. Its influence was a sectional rather than a mass one, thus it never inspired mural painters. It found some pictorial representation, however, in the seemingly unlikely source of the painter Jim Fitzpatrick, whose intricate Celtic designs and romantic images of macho warriors and seductive Celtic maidens were until then judged to be the epitome of nationalist mythologizing. Fitzpatrick drew the cover for the 1986 edition of *The Cruthin*, a depiction of Cuchulain defending Ulster against the invading Celts. But no loyalist mural painter was inspired to copy Fitzpatrick's imagery in the way a republican mural artist, Gerard Kelly, was to imitate him one year later.

A similar although lesser historical revisionism occurred in relation to the Red Hand of Ulster, a traditional unionist symbol in Northern Ireland. Originally the symbol had belonged to the O'Neills, the rulers of the north, whose uprising in 1641 had almost led to the sudden death of the Elizabethan plantation. Why, then, should a nationalist symbol be accepted by unionists? The UVF of the 1970s justified it in terms reminiscent of those used by Adamson and the Young Unionist Council.

> The Red Hand of the O'Neills has been adopted by the Ulster Loyalist population as a symbol of their separate identity with the rest of Ireland. In keeping with the traditions of the red right hand, we could do no better than adopt the war cry of the O'Neills—"lamh dearg abu—the Red Hand to Victory!" (*Combat* 1, no. 8 [May] 1974)

An offshoot of the UVF took the name Red Hand Commandos, and the symbol became a common image in loyalist murals in the 1980s.

But one wonders if everyone who used the symbol was aware of the subtleties of the revisionist argument. For example, in Inverna Street, South Belfast, the local defence group,

Inverna Street, 1983. Red Hand of Ulster and initials of Roden Street Defence Group.

Roden Street Defence, painted its initials RSD beneath a large red hand. The hand is dripping blood, showing that these mural painters seem to have been following the other supposed origin of the symbol. Myth has it that when two chieftains rushed to claim land near Lough Neagh, they agreed that whoever touched the land first would rule it. One chieftain cut off his left hand and threw it from the boat onto land, thus winning the race.

The Red Hand was not the only traditional symbol in the murals of the 1980s. King Billy continued to appear with predictable uniformity, qualified, as usual, only by the artist's skill. The most ornate mural is in North Street, Ballymena, with King Billy, unusually, on a piebald horse. It is also unusual because the mural itself is circular rather than rectangular. Most of the King Billys are of average quality, such as that in Lindsay Street, which depicts a dead or dying Jacobite soldier and mixes portraiture and action painting; the one in Irish Street in Derry's Waterside, which also contains a landscape; and the one on the Shore Road, Belfast, which only has a horse and rider, without any attempt to represent the water of the river Boyne. Similar representations appear in the Windy Hall housing estate near Coleraine—the only embellishment being that the horse's feet are submerged in shallow water—and in an entry behind houses in Severn Street, in which one of the worst King Billys for

Irish Street, Derry. King Billy crossing the Boyne.

Off Severn Street, 1987. King Billy crossing the Boyne.

Shore Road, 1984. King Billy crossing the Boyne.

which a photographic record exists was painted in 1987, being no more lifelike than a puppet on a wooden fairground horse.

Much more common throughout the 1980s was the representation of flags.[12] The heraldic grandeur in most cases could be taken concomitantly as a harking to past glories as well as being at odds with current confused realities. The murals reveal a false confidence. In some cases the Union Jack is the only flag represented, as in the mural in the unlikely setting of a wall of a public lavatory in Donemana, County Derry. In others the Ulster flag is given equal space, as in a large mural in Bond Street, Derry or an equally large and ornate mural in Hopewell Avenue. Some murals contain the Scottish flag of St. Andrew, including the memorial to the Reverend Robert Bradford, MP, killed by the IRA in 1981. Beneath a painted arch bearing the slogan that had graced the traditional Twelfth arch in the same street for years ("Cemented with Love"), the flags were draped "in loving memory" of the local MP.

Despite their grandeur, flags in murals did not match what republicans at their best were producing at the same time. Republicans had certain advantages. They could make international connections in their murals, with the PLO (Palestine

Windy Hall, near Coleraine, County Derry, 1988. King Billy crossing the Boyne.

Donemana, County Derry, 1983. Red Hand of Ulster and Union Jack.

Hopewell Avenue, 1984. Flags, crown, and Red Hand of Ulster; "In God Our Trust."

Bond Street, Derry, 1982. Flags, crown, and Red Hand of Ulster.

Percy Place, 1984. Links between Ulster and Scotland; flags, crown, and Red Hand of Ulster.

Bond Street, Derry, 1982. Canadian and Australian flags, crown, and Red Hand of Ulster.

Liberation Organization) or ANC (African National Congress), for example, or borrow images from other revolutions regardless of how badly the analogy between their revolution and the others limped in the eyes of political scientists. Loyalists could stress their Britishness, but at times this was a precarious connection, as shown when the Union Jack often shared space with or was replaced by the Ulster flag and other flags. Some murals referred to the cultural and political links between Scotland and Northern Ireland by including the flag of St. Andrew; interestingly, in at least one case there is a crown but no Union Jack, declaring "Ulster—Scotland—United We Stand." Although Scottish sympathizers have helped the loyalist cause by marching and supplying weapons, there is not quite the same romanticism in such a connection as in a shared political ideology with anti-imperialist struggles in, say, Nicaragua or South Africa. In Bond Street, Derry, the political isolation of unionism is encapsulated in a mural of two flags, Australian and Canadian, on either side of the Red Hand of Ulster; the connections are to an empire that was, but is now gone.[13]

THE ANGLO-IRISH AGREEMENT AND BEYOND

If the story of loyalist murals had ended in the early 1980s, then it would have seemed fair to predict that the tradition was in a deep slump from which recovery was unlikely. Such a conclusion would have been premature. A strong hint of change to come occurred in July 1984 when a young Shankill Road man, Alan Skillen, decided to paint murals. In an incredible rush of activity he painted seven large murals on gable walls in Percy Place in the few weeks leading up to the Twelfth. Percy Place is a small cul-de-sac with few gable walls. When Skillen was finished and numerous other decorations had been added—an Orange arch, bunting, painted curbstones, and lamp posts—it was impossible

Percy Place, 1984. "Shankill Supports Loyalist Prisoners."

to turn in any direction in the street without encountering a visual avalanche of loyalist symbolism.

Skillen's themes were traditional: one is a King Billy of mediocre quality, the legs of the horse too short and the King's body too large; another mural depicts simply a bible and a crown. Another displays Union Jacks, a loyalist shield containing the emblems of the UVF, UDA, Red Hand Commandos, and the Young Citizen Volunteers (YCV; youth wing of the UVF); and also adds confidently (and in this sense is different from an earlier mural on the subject already referred to that meekly asks the viewer to "re-

Percy Place, 1984. King Billy crossing the Boyne.

member the loyalist prisoners"): "Shankill supports all the loyalist prisoners." It is clear from this mural that Skillen's motivation was not solely decorative, despite his claim to a journalist that he was trying "to brighten up the area and stop people writing on the walls" (*Belfast Telegraph*, 3 July 1984). A number of the murals are unequivocably loyalist, not only supporting loyalist prisoners, but also the armed struggle as a result of which they had become prisoners. Thus one mural, copied from an album cover, shows a uniformed and armed loyalist volunteer holding an Ulster flag and posing in front of a large representation of a Northern Ireland cut off entirely from the South and Britain. There is no Union Jack, no symbol other than the crown on the Ulster flag to proclaim a unionist as opposed to a loyalist political identity. Commentators such as Rees (1985) and Nairn (1977), who had seen the rise of Ulster nationalism in the UWC Strike ten years earlier, would have had their theories confirmed by the symbolism of this mural. Close by another mural praises the armed struggle. Again there is no specific unionist symbolism; an armed and uniformed loyalist volunteer poses on one knee in front of loyalist flags. Beneath him is the emblem of the UVF and above the proclamation, both a factual statement and a statement of intent: "This is loyalist West Belfast." The territorial claim here becomes significant when one remembers that loyalists launched an attack on nearby nationalist streets and burned hundreds of homes from this exact area before redevelopment in August 1969. The spires of St. Peter's Catholic Pro-Cathedral on the lower Falls Road are visible behind the mural, a few hundred yards away across the "peace line."

At the same time as Skillen was painting his murals, another, also copied from an album cover, appeared at Ainsworth Avenue. The life-size armed volunteer stands at the entrance to the loyalist streets facing the nationalist area across the road; whether his stance is one of defense or intimidation depends, in the literal geographical sense, on one's viewpoint.

Thus July 1984 had an intense representation of loyalist armed struggle that had not been witnessed previously. There were few such murals before then, one which has already been referred to—the bust modelled of Gusty Spence in

Percy Place, 1984. Loyalist sentry with Ulster flag.

Percy Place, 1984. Armed loyalist.

Derry's Fountain area. Also in Derry, in the Waterside, a masked and armed volunteer dressed in a combat jacket appears in a mural. In Belfast two very poorly executed murals in the Woodvale area depict the armed struggle—one showing the partial bust of a masked and uniformed UVF man, the other the kneeling silhouettes of three armed volunteers with weapons, flags, and the emblems of the UVF, UDA, and YCV. Finally, a mural on an internal wall of the UDA headquarters in Gawn Street contains a number of standard symbols, as well as references to loyalist prisoners, a Red Hand giving a victory sign, and two armed volunteers, who are unmasked and look almost indistinguishable from British army personnel. In short, despite the loyalist paramilitary activity going on for almost

Waterside, Derry, 1981. Masked and uniformed loyalist.

Gawn Street, Headquarters of Ulster Defence Association. Flags and armed loyalists.

Woodvale area. Bust of armed loyalist.

Woodvale area. Loyalist volunteers, weapons, and emblems of Ulster Defence Association, Ulster Volunteer Force, and Young Citizen Volunteers.

twenty years, there was little mural representation of that involvement as late as 1984.

A major reason for this gap is that it was difficult to portray most of loyalist military activity in heroic terms. In this sense, republicans have an advantage: their clarity of ideology, cause, and target lends itself to romantic and heroic representation. But the bulk of loyalist military activity has involved the assassination of lone and unarmed nationalists. The problem for loyalist mural painters is how to portray the groups involved in heroic form. One solution, only used rarely, is to paint heroic murals anyway. Thus, in Ohio Street, North Belfast, one mural shows two UVF volunteers firing from behind a wall; no specific target is identified pictorially, but the adjoining caption states: "The UVF reserve the right to strike at republican targets where and when the opportunity arises."

Identifying republicans is clearly the problem, leading in many cases to the easier solution of targeting any nationalist. Nearby on the main Crumlin Road, beside the symbols of a number of organizations linked to the UDA, two UFF men run across hills firing weapons at an unspecified target. The viewer knows, however, that the main activity of one of the organizations identified in these murals, the UFF (Ulster Freedom Fighters), has been the assassination of nationalists (Dillon and Lehane 1973). Thus the heroic images in these murals are much removed from the reality of loyalist military action.

An alternative solution is to present armed

Ohio Street, 1987. Ulster Volunteer Force in action.

Severn Street, 1987. Armed loyalists.

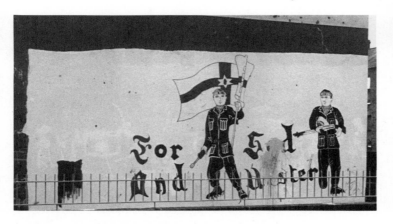

Rosebank Street. Armed loyalists.

Doagh Road, 1988. Armed loyalist, Red Hand of Ulster, and LPA (Loyalist Prisoners Association).

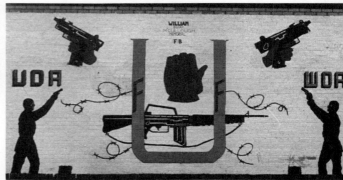

Ohio Street, 1987. Armed loyalists, Ulster Freedom Fighters.

volunteers as symbols along with flags and other emblems. Weapons became plentiful in murals after 1984, but they usually are not pointed at anyone. Similarly, the volunteers are not active, but merely posed, a symbol among symbols. This is the case in a mural in Severn Street that shows three armed and uniformed but unmasked volunteers, as well as another in Rosebank Street, partially copied from the same

Lisburn, County Antrim, 1987. Armed member of Ulster Freedom Fighters and flags.

source, an album sleeve of loyalist songs. In Rathcoole, beside a crown and a large Red Hand of Ulster, an armed loyalist is posed as a vigilant sentry. Even when the volunteers are firing guns, as in an Ohio Street mural celebrating the UDA, UFF, and WDA (Woodvale Defence Association), the volley is harmless. Murals of this form can be read easily within the common portrayal of loyalism as being merely a defense against republican aggression. But the murals are threatening, too, and are frequently intended to be. One mural in Lisburn proves the point. Although poorly executed, the armed UFF figure in balaclava and combat jacket is obviously threatening to any nationalist lingering in this loyalist area. This is no mere Halloween masquerade, a message enhanced by the fact that the year before this mural was painted a nationalist electrician working on houses in the town had been assassinated by the UFF.

Why was there such a revival in loyalist mural painting after 1984? Why in that revival was there such a proliferation of militaristic images? The answers are linked. In 1985, the London and Dublin governments signed the Anglo-Irish Agreement.[14] Hailed as a historic step on the road to solving "the Northern Ireland problem," the Agreement was rejected outright by union-

ists on two grounds. First, they were never consulted about the Agreement, whereas the nationalists, through the SDLP (Social Democratic and Labour Party), had a line into ongoing discussions resulting from their contacts with the Dublin government. Second, by appearing to give the South a say in the internal affairs of the North, especially in the administration of justice, the Agreement was anathema to Northern unionists. Consequently, unionist opposition to the Agreement was vociferous. Through marches, rallies, council boycotts, and the like, the Official Unionists and the Democratic Unionists reached a level of unity of purpose and action that had eluded them for some time.

Part of the opposition to the Agreement was an increase in loyalist militarism. Although unionist politicians claimed the Agreement was the beginning of the final sell-out of Ulster, the loyalist paramilitary groups prepared to defend Ulster against sell-out. And as attack is said to be the surest form of defense, it was inevitable that lone, unarmed nationalists again would be prime targets.

Initially, response to the Anglo-Irish Agreement on unionist walls consisted solely of graffiti. On the Limestone Road, Tigers Bay First Flute Band issued an ultimatum that was arresting no less for its contortion of geography as for its political conviction: "Ireland stay out of our country." In Ballysillan, in a reference to the RUC's involvement in policing loyalist protests to the Agreement, one witty graffiti artist wrote: "Support a united Ireland. Join the RUC." Coining the slogan of the coal merchants' association

The Fountain, Derry, 1987. "No Surrender."

*The Fountain, Derry, 1987. The Pope waving a loy-
alist scarf, flags, and emblems of Ulster Defence Association, Ulster Defence Force, Ulster Freedom
Fighters, and Loyalist Prisoners Association.*

*Lurgan, County Armagh, 1987. Armed loyalist de-
fends woman and Ulster; "United We Stand."*

and referring to the petrol bombing of the homes
of RUC personnel, a common graffito was "Join
the RUC and come home to a real fire." But in
time the images became pictorial, bringing together loyalist symbolism, the slogan of unionist
opposition—"Ulster Says No"—and militaristic
imagery. In the Fountain area of Derry, residents
made it clear that, although they were "still
under siege" and isolated in a predominantly

nationalist city, they would not surrender to the
Anglo-Irish Agreement. Across the street from
this mural is a wittier, although poorly painted
one (copied from a Rathcoole mural of some
years previously); even the Pope "says No" to
the Anglo-Irish Agreement, as he is shown waving a scarf with the word "Ulster" on it. In
Lurgan, against the background of a Northern
Ireland in the form of an Ulster flag, an armed
man protects a woman from unseen aggressors;
"United we stand" says the accompanying slogan. In Meekon Street all the symbols come together—the flags, the armed defenders of today
and yesteryear, the Ulster "colleen" (referred to
below); in addition, a Red Hand of Ulster has
magically sprouted feet and dances on an Irish
tricolor in protest at the Anglo-Irish Agreement.

An additional incentive to mural painters was
that 1987 was the 75th anniversary of the formation of the UVF. Some murals appeared that
could be read as solely historical in content and
commemorative in intent. A remarkably capable
one in Dervock, County Antrim, circular in
shape and soothing rather than aggressive, not
least by its careful use of shades of blue, depicts
three Ulster Division men going over the top at
the Battle of the Somme. On Albertbridge Road
was an equally carefully painted commemorative
mural to the men of the Ulster Division (previously the UVF) who had fallen at the Battle of
the Somme; gray and red, it portrays a sense of

*Shankill Road, 1987. Motorized division of the Ulster
Volunteer Force, 1912.*

poignancy, and the figures are the most stylistic in any loyalist mural. On the Shankill Road some young artists from a nearby government-sponsored youth and community workshop attempted less successfully to depict the motorized division of the 1912 UVF, with the partially recognizable bust of Edward Carson, the leader of unionist opposition to the Home Rule Bill. In this latter case, the artists were at pains to point out in an interview that their mural was "only cultural." But the links between the historical and contemporary UVF were there to be made. They were spelt out clearly in at least one mural done by the same artists further down Shankill Road where posing UVF men of two generations are depicted, and continuity is emphasized by the use of the words "then" and "now." The same point of apostolic succession is made in a mural in Dee Street in which the three dates 1912, 1916, and 1987 appear over the three figures: an original UVF man, a soldier of the Ulster Division, and a contemporary UVF man, respectively. The most forceful mural is in Craven Street, off the Shankill Road. On the front wall of a club associated with the UVF, the Battle of the Somme and the struggle of the current UVF are shown as part of the one loyalist fight, even down to depicting the point cited earlier by Tim Pat Coogan, that the "UVF prisoners of war" called their huts after the battlefields where the Ulster Division had fought 71 years before. Fi-

Dee Street, 1987. Ulster Volunteer Force, 1912–1987; "Ulster Will Fight."

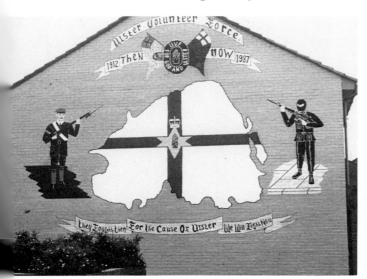

Shankill Road, 1987. 75th anniversary of foundation of Ulster Volunteer Force.

nally, on the back of the same building, a 1914 postcard (which appeared the previous year in Killen 1986, p. 72) was reproduced as a mural. Its unusual loyalist symbolism portrays an armed woman; even more unusual she is depicted as a stereotypical Irish colleen representing not Ireland, but Ulster. Holding a gun, she says: "Deserted! Well—I can stand alone."

The loyalist armed struggle was out in the open, blessed as a result of its connection with a previous struggle. Because the latter was deemed a crucial and respectable part of unionist history and identity, it legitimized the portrayal of the current armed struggle. After the links with 1912–16 were made in some murals, other murals could celebrate the current armed struggle in its own right. In Highfield a set of small

Highfield Community Centre, 1986. Loyalist emblems: Ulster Volunteer Force. Ulster Defence Association, Young Citizen Volunteers, and Red Hand Commandos.

Dee Street, 1987. Roll of Honor of Ulster Defence Association dead.

Leroy Street, 1986. Roll of Honor of Ulster Volunteer Force prisoners and dead in action.

murals on boards over the entrance to a community center serve as a "who's who" of loyalist paramilitaries—UVF, YCV, UDA, RHC—while in Ballysillan an awkward mural serves as a tribute to UVF men from the area serving time in prison for their military activity by listing their names in a crude heraldic design. In Dee Street a tomblike memorial mural also lists names, this time of loyalist volunteers who had been killed in action. Loyalist murals have come a long way from King Billy.

CONCLUSION

It has been argued throughout this chapter that both the unionist confidence in the early part of this century and its confusion later in the century have had their cultural effects. In that sense loyalist murals, in their content and quantity, provide some measure of the current state of unionist identity and politics.

It is important to reemphasize how severe the confusion of unionism has been over the last two decades. Not only have many of the bulwarks of the old unionist state, including the devolved parliament at Stormont, been eased out of the picture as a result of direct British reinvolvement in the political process, but the seige mentality of unionism has been further fuelled by numerous apparent attempts to placate rebellious nationalists. As far as unionists are concerned, that many nationalists could less easily point to ways in which British reformism has substantially bettered their lot is not the point. The "enemies of Ulster" have been wooed and mollycoddled through a variety of events, including the disbandment of the B Specials, the prorogation of Stormont, the power-sharing executive of 1974, the legalization of Sinn Féin, the failure to allow the security forces a "free hand" in the pursuit of republican activists, the Anglo-Irish Agreement of 1985, and so on.

One aspect of this increasing sense of isolation for unionists is the differential assessment made by nationalists and unionists of their respective local communities. For unionists it was not merely that the state was *their* state. Each local area vied with others to have the largest bonfire, the smartest dressed flute band, the most ornate arch, and so on. But such symbols and celebrations were not only local. Each local area was a link in the unionist chain. By parading what were regarded by the dominant group in Northern Ireland society as civic symbols, the local area became the state writ small; the symbols and artifacts had a wider-than-local political significance. For nationalists, on the other hand, the local community was a ghetto, the only place where nationalist culture could be freely expressed in the absence of access to state institutions and civic symbols. But as a ghetto, it was not merely experienced in a negative manner; at times, especially as the 1970s progressed, it also became the springboard for political activity—as community action or republican military operations—directed against the state.

By this point, however, with the British reforms making more and more changes at least in appearance, unionists increasingly found themselves confined in ways they had never been when they had controlled the state. The community ceased to be the state writ small, because in many ways it was no longer *their* state. Thus the community experience was, in many ways, a negative one for unionists, a lowering of horizons from the days when the whole state was their home ground. In a strange reversal of roles, by the early 1980s the unionists lacked con-

Unionist anti–Anglo-Irish Agreement poster, 1986; "Unionist Solidarity."

Severn Street, 1987. Red Hand protecting Ulster; "Ulster is British."

Doagh Road, 1988. Clenched Red Hand of Ulster and emblem of Ulster Defence Force.

Tulleevin Drive, 1988. Red Hand of Ulster dances on Irish tricolor; "No Surrender."

fidence while the nationalists never felt so self-assured.

During the 1980s, unionists have continued to search for symbols to replace or buttress those damaged through direct rule and the Anglo-Irish Agreement—going back to the mythology of the pre-Celtic Cruthin, reinterpreting events and personages usually claimed only by nationalists, or scavenging for symbols as far afield as Aquino's slogan of "people power" in the Philippines or the banner of Solidarity in Poland,

unashamedly copied by the Official Unionist Party for an anti–Anglo-Irish Agreement poster. To date, no overarching unifying symbols have been found to replace those lost.

The point can be emphasized by considering the different possible uses of one particular symbol, the Red Hand of Ulster. It can be used as a unionist symbol, as in one mural off Severn Street; the Red Hand envelopes Ulster and the slogan proclaims that "Ulster is British"; the union with Britain is thus Ulster's surest protection. On the other hand, the Red Hand can be a loyalist symbol, either one of defiance, as in a Rathcoole mural of an almost comic style fist dripping blood, or of ridicule, as in those murals in which the hand has feet and dances on the Irish tricolor and two fingers gesture in a victory sign. "Ulster is British" and "Ulster has been betrayed by Britain" are notions that together can be seen as separate themes throughout loyalist murals.

The confusion of unionism has had specific effects on young people. Bell (1986b, p. 10) has argued that

> Contemporary loyalist street culture with its political folk festivals and parades . . . and its symbolic demarcation of a Protestant sense of territory via display of ethnic iconography (wall and kerb paintings, graffiti, flag and insignia display), has in its informal activities beyond the hierarchical control of the "official" Orange organisations been the almost exclusive preserve of male working class teenagers.

But, he continues, these young loyalists are not merely aping the styles and actions of their elders. In taking over the cultural practices of adult loyalists, they have in many ways transformed them into a specifically loyalist youth culture. Thus the young people have revived and transformed the practice of band parades, the specific focus of Bell's study, as well as revived mural painting. In doing so, often these young people have acted on their own, beyond the influence of the traditional adult loyalist organizations such as the Orange Order. Even the new and more militant loyalist paramilitary organizations that found many recruits among the young, often found their youth groups hard to control, as Nelson (1984, p. 174) notes regarding the relationship between the UVF and the Young

Crumlin Road, 1987. Young loyalist mural painters at work.

Hogarth Street (Tiger's Bay). Tiger.

Doagh Road, 1988. British bulldog.

Citizen Volunteers (YCV).

Like youth subcultures elsewhere, Bell (1986b, p. 18) argues, the specifically loyalist youth subculture can be best understood as

> an attempt to sustain a sense of "community" and collective identity in a situation where traditional structures and sentiments of communality have been eroded . . .

Because it has been adults who have lost the sense of community and young males in particular who strive to recapture it, this lends the specific youth focus to current cultural practices.

Young people make up the "blood and thunder" bands; they are behind the revival of loyalist mural painting, a revival seen not just in the quantity of murals but also in the militaristic content of many recent ones. The influence of youth also is seen in the willingness of the artists to break from traditional forms and themes, borrowing from op art, cartoon, comic, and other styles in a wider popular culture for specifically loyalist purposes, be it a British bulldog in a Rathcoole mural or the growling tiger of Tigers Bay. Moreover, it is not surprising perhaps that in searching for symbols the young mural artists have returned to the old stories with a new sense of identification, in at least one instance commemorating the young loyalists of a previous generation, the apprentice boys who shut the gates of Derry against the Jacobites one year before the Battle of the Boyne.

2

"Cooling Out the Community"? Belfast's Community Mural Program

INTRODUCTION

IN HIS EPIC ACCOUNT OF THE COMMUNITY MURAL movement in the United States in the 1960s and 1970s, Barnett (1984, p. 19) argues that the movement derived from the convergence of three elements: the "yearning of artists for roots . . . of working people for means of expression . . . and of communities for control over their own existence." Many artists had become totally alienated from the closed world of fine art. Foremost among them were black artists, because the world of fine art was also racist. At the same time, the 1960s saw an upsurge of grass-roots political action over a wide range of issues. In addition to a national politics of antiwar and antiracist agitation, there was also a resurgence of community politics; that is, action by local people on issues directly affecting their local areas. Given all these elements, Barnett argues, it was no coincidence that artists, particularly black artists, turned to painting murals for communities as a way out of their alienation and frustration. Nor was it coincidental that communities turned to art as a weapon in their struggle over the quality of life in local areas.

After the community arts movement blossomed, organization and funding problems arose. Funding frequently came from government agencies at the federal, state, or city level. Barnett's (1984, p. 424) conclusion regarding federal funding of community arts can be validly applied to much state and city funding: "the principal motive for . . . funding for inner-city arts was to 'cool out' ghetto and barrio youth." This is not to say that the state, at whatever level, always had its way. It emphasizes, however, that the merging of the interests of certain artists, communities, and the state meant that the overall effect often counterposed financial survival and radicalism; the more of one, the less of the other.

It is tempting to apply an identical analysis to the experience of community arts in Belfast in the late 1970s and early 1980s. Although the artistic community was small, there were undoubtedly artists who were alienated from the closed world of museums and exhibitions and who wanted to say something valuable to ordinary people. In addition, there was a strong community movement in Belfast in the 1970s; surely such a movement would have been eager to use artistic forms to propagate its arguments and would have turned easily to the alienated artists seeking a social outlet for their art. Finally, given that the state was the main sponsor of community arts and that murals were directed solely toward ghetto areas that by that time had seen a decade of violence, it could be concluded that the motivation for being involved in financing community arts was in "cooling out" violent and politically aware urban youth.

Although superficially similar to the U.S. case, the brief appearance of state-sponsored community arts in Belfast had different origins, motivations, and effects. There were few "socially aware" artists and even fewer who offered their services to the community movement; in fact, all the artists who worked on the state-sponsored community arts scheme were students at Belfast's College of Art and Design.

Moreover, although the community arts experiment was channelled partially through the community movement, that movement had lost much of its vitality by the time the state began sponsoring murals in 1977. Finally, by that point in time Belfast had experienced a decade of military repression and guerrilla activity, much of the violence being most severe in the ghettoes where the murals were painted. But the "cooling out" of these areas had been pursued consistently by the British militarily. Murals were not an important part of that counter-insurgency activity.

The origins of and motivation for the state-sponsored community arts intervention must be sought in an entirely different area, namely, in the political and economic pressures on British politicians in the Northern Ireland Office that led them to engage in low level environmental improvement.

ART, ARTISTS AND THE "TROUBLES"

Surveying the then current state of the visual arts in Ireland in 1983, Lambert (1983, p. 203) concluded:

> In a divided Ireland the arts continue to be a unifying force because they transcend social status, income levels and political and religious differences.

Far from conveying the notion of art as classless, nonsectarian, and totally objective, this conclusion reveals the middle-class bias of the art establishment in Ireland. The keystone of the establishment's self-defined identity is the notion of artists as transcendent beings. In relation to the North, this ideology becomes a justification for ignoring what is happening in the real world, especially if it is happening to working-class people. If artists have been a "unifying force," which is debatable, it is not because they have somehow brought people, other than themselves, together but because they have studiously ignored the real divisions among people in the North; namely, "social status, income levels and religious and political differences."

Despite the "troubles," it is remarkable how little visual artists have descended from the dizzy heights of "pure art" to comment on the world of insurgency and counter-insurgency. There are a few exceptions: Patric Coogan, whose subtle allusions to violence and the fear it engenders among ordinary people might be lost on the uninitiated; Brendan Ellis (Ellis 1985), with his bleak urban landscapes and discomforting images of people as either victims or survivors; Joe McWilliams, who has attempted more directly to portray political events and people, whether Orange Order marches or uniformed paramilitaries; Dermot Seymour (Seymour 1986), with his apparently incongruous juxtapositioning of the artifacts of war and rural idyll; and John Kindness (Kindness and Davies 1985), whose apparently flippant cartoon style conceals pointed political comment just below the surface. But in the overall panorama of visual arts in the North, these are exceptions to the rule, as summarized by Catto (1977, p. 130): "Most artists in Ulster tend to produce work which has little relationship to the troubles." One of those artists, McWilliams (1982, p. 7), agrees: "With few exceptions Northern Irish art is unrelated to our present troubles."

Catto (1977, p. 130) adds that such lack of social comment "could be construed by artists in other countries as a sign of weakness." After all, in other areas of the arts in the North the silence has not been so deafening. Poets and playwrights, for example, have frequently attempted to write about the North, its "troubles," and their position in relation to repression, resistance, sectarian division, and so on. It is true there are two schools of thought on this among poets and playwrights, but those arguing for social relevance, indeed for the artist as provider of intellectual leadership, have stated their case loudly and well.[1] No such developed debate exists in the visual arts. Catto (1977, p. 130) attempts to explain.

> I imagine that the average Ulster artist . . . would claim that the troubles are merely a temporary aberration and that he doesn't need to produce scenes of bombing and shooting to prove that he is sensitive to what is happening.

McWilliams's (1982, p. 7) explanation of artistic silence is more substantial:

> It appears that detachment rather than involvement is a pre-requisite for any art activity which seems to emerge from or relate to the socio-political tensions in the North . . . Art emerging from the "eye of the storm" might very well produce more force than feeling. It might even produce propagandist pictures, owing more to politics than to painting.[2]

That one of the few artists known for socially aware art in the North should emphatically endorse such notions as "detachment equals art, involvement equals propaganda," and should counterpose "art" to "nationalist" or "unionist realism" shows the extent to which the ideological conception of "pure art" imbues the artistic profession in the North.

Given that unanimity, any disagreements within the profession reveal less an irreconcilable difference between two ideologies than an internal debate conducted within the one ideological universe. To take one example: in November 1978 an exhibition of paintings entitled "Art for Society," held originally at the Whitechapel Gallery in London (Serota et al. 1978), ran into trouble when it was scheduled to open at Belfast's Ulster Museum. The press reported that some Museum attendants objected to some of the paintings because they were too political.

Actually, the workforce at the Museum is predominantly unionist[3] and is likely to object to anything that might be construed as antiunionist or pronationalist. Thus, when DUP councillor Billy Dickson, a supervisor at the Museum, said that "in no way could the men man the gallery, as they would have had to put up with a lot of abuse from the public" (*Belfast Newsletter*, 8 November 1978), he spoke in a code that any resident of the North could understand; for "public" read "unionists" and for "men" read "guardians of unionist ideals." The offending exhibits were removed and shown in another gallery. But the Museum trustees attempted to defuse the whole affair by stating that they had made the decision to cancel the exhibition, not based on objections from attendants, but because they had a duty as a public body to be nonpolitical (*Belfast Newsletter*, 10 November 1978). From their point of view, for the artist to openly take up political themes was unacceptable. The artists could not agree and argued that artists have the right to deal with political themes if it is done in a detached, nonpartisan, and nonpropagandist way. The row between trustees and artists was conducted at the level of the right of the pure artist to freedom of expression. At no point did the artists speak of their duty to make social comment; instead, the debate was in terms of the bourgeois ideal of individual freedom. The artists' difference with the trustees was over the latter's cautiousness and conservatism in interpreting their duty as public caretakers of the arts, and not a head-on collision between notions of detachment versus commitment in art.

A similar sense of fundamental ideological agreement emerges when one considers the activities of the Arts Council of Northern Ireland and criticisms made of it. The Arts Council Board has mostly interpreted its extremely general brief—"to increase the accessibility of the fine arts to the public"—in the safest way, sponsoring those things defined as "high art." Twenty percent of the Council's budget goes toward the upkeep of the Ulster Orchestra. Belfast's Grand Opera House takes another substantial slice of each annual budget. As a result, the visual arts end up as a poor cousin, with only three bursaries per annum, each valued at £5,000, and an often derisory purchasing scheme that enabled the Council to spend the vast sum of £7,670 in the financial year 1983–84 on buying finished works of art by visual artists. Such criticisms of the Arts Council as these made by Walker (1985) reveal the fundamentally conservative bourgeois bias of the Arts Council in practice. Walker proposes a more democratic structure for the Arts Council and the establishment of a clearly stated policy. These innovations, she argues (1985, p. 27), would force the Council to liaise with the art community and the wider public and flush it out of its current isolation wherein it is "communicating with no one but itself."

However, the thrust of Walker's argument, if implemented, need be no more than a change from a conservative bourgeois bias to a more liberal bourgeois bias. She does not question the supremacy of fine art in the Arts Council's raison d'etre, but merely demands that certain fine arts (the visual arts) receive more funding. When she speaks of the wider public, she implies that section of the public that consumes fine art, as defined. But there are more fundamental criticisms that can be made of the Arts Council and its activities. Why does the Arts Council accept solely dominant definitions of *art* as to make its activities irrelevant to vast sections of the population? Why is it assumed that the world is divided into producers of art and consumers of art, thus ensuring that the cultural activities of many members of society, particularly the working class, are not regarded as worthy of encouragement and sponsorship? Why does the Arts Council Board studiously avoid considering ways it can encourage more socially aware art or art that is politically radical? In short, the major criticism that can be made of the Arts Council relates to its bourgeois nature rather than its conservatism. By not asking these questions, Walker reveals that her concern is that of the professional artist and her criticisms of the Arts Council are of its failure to fully encourage and envigorate all sections of the profession. To paraphrase her own statement, her criticisms are a case of the profession communicating with itself.

All in all, the arts profession in the North, whether established or critical of the establishment, moves in the same ideological space, accepting standard definitions of art and orthodox distinctions between art and propaganda, detachment and involvement. This ideology is so fundamental to the profession that it emerges early in the artistic career and is taught religiously, albeit as a partially "hidden curriculum," to all students.

Arts training takes place at the College of Art and Design in Belfast (an integral part of the University of Ulster since the mid-1980s). It is clear from the course content, as well as from the artistic output of the students, that consideration of Northern Ireland society and politics is mostly avoided. Of course, this is not justified as cowardice or conservatism, but by defining the local as "parochial." In contradistinction, art colleges are concerned with conveying the "universal." The artistic imagination is said to transcend the merely local or contemporary. However, that imagination does give rise to different styles and the assimilation of those styles that are in fashion becomes the core of artistic training. This causes problems; for a start, as McLennan (1985, p. 21), a lecturer at the Art College, points out,

> because Ireland was and is dominated by an (ex) imperial power, standards were determined in that other country—England. The High Culture was English and the common traditions were subjugated.

That would not be problematic if art was currently in the forefront of discovering and encouraging local traditions as a foil to the weight of "cultural imperialism." But this does not occur at the Art College.

> Both course content and structures focus too much on international developments. There is overmuch concern with apeing internationally validated style.

Adare (1986), an exstudent of the Art College, agrees that art education thus becomes not the development under supervision of one's own artistic imagination, as the ideal would have it, but the faithful mimicking of the fad. The ultimate mortal sin is failure to conform, either in style or, more crucially, in the content of one's art. With *local* coterminous with *parochial*, failure to copy the internationally legitimated styles and themes is to engage in an activity other than art.

> Certainly, the problems of Belfast and the troubles of Northern Ireland stayed well outside the walls of

Northern Ireland's only Art College; within, the siege mentality reigned. A sure way to get nowhere was to try to incorporate some of what was happening in one's own life outside into the work you were doing/wanted to do inside. There must be few such places in the world where so much was going on outside and so little of it manifesting itself within. Visitors from other countries assumed all this would find expression in the work produced in the College; they sought in vain. Why? People who (for instance) were (as you knew) furious Republicans painted simpering pink canvases with twee little Miroesque blobs, etc. There was no reflection of what they were thinking or feeling, and talking about, most of the time. . . ." (Adare 1986, p. 36)

Adare (1986, p. 37) is clear in her conclusion: "Close the art colleges and let no one fear the fate of 'Art'." But McLennan (1985, p. 21) is content with a more timid conclusion:

The study of art and social context go hand-in-hand, though in Belfast local subject matter is often overlooked. This is a pity and ought to be questioned.

Weak as it is, the conclusion seems too strong for the author, who immediately justifies his proposal in terms of a much used and practically infallible mechanism, invocation of the ideal of harmonious community relations. "In this context every healing agent counts. Art is one and is not used sufficiently." In a society in which the churches, state, and media have conspired to present everything from the Belfast Marathon to the activities of world champion boxer Barry McGuigan as exercises in community relations, who can fault McLennan's rendition of art as missionary work? In an entirely different way it could be said that David Speir, also a lecturer at the Art College, had a sense of the "missionary" purpose of art. His concern to "bring art into the lives of ordinary people" (letter to author, 29 November 1985) was both more orthodox and practical than McLennan's ethereal idealism.

Speir was concerned with the alienation of modern life, with

people living in areas that were often very deprived in every sense, often lacking any feature of any kind, more particularly, oddly enough, in the more modern estates than in the old ones" (transcript of taped interview with Julian Watson, 1982).

He saw community art as having some ability to humanize what he described as a "jungle" through making "works of imaginative quality . . . visible to a large number of people who otherwise would never have experienced anything like that." Speir's concerns were profoundly orthodox, especially when looked at alongside some more radical justifications of community art elsewhere in the world; art was locked up in museums and galleries where it had no effect on the people who needed it most. If they could not go to the galleries, the galleries would go to them. Although it was mainstream, Speir's initiative fed into a program that was proportionately the largest state-sponsored mural scheme up to that point anywhere in the United Kingdom and that was well received by artists and community muralists elsewhere.

However, the existence and, in its own terms, success of Belfast's community mural scheme cannot be attributed to the vision or artistic missionary zeal of one man. Speir's ideas took on form because they matched the political and economic needs of the time.

THE PURSUIT OF "NORMALITY"

After taking over direct rule of Northern Ireland in 1972, British ministers faced two major crises, one political, the other economic.

The political crisis was clear in the need to take over direct rule in the first place. British policy since then has been based on the principle of attempting to contain Northern Ireland's troubles, first within Northern Ireland and second within nationalist ghettoes in Northern Ireland (O'Dowd, Rolston, and Tomlinson 1982). By the second half of the 1970s, this strategy involved a sophisticated approach that led to the "Ulsterization" of security; that is, shifting the burden of responsibility from the British army to the local Royal Ulster Constabulary and Ulster Defence Regiment. Also crucial was the policy of "criminalization," that is, the phasing out of internment and special category status for politically motivated prisoners. With a police force at the forefront of security and the absence of political prisoners, Northern Ireland could be presented as a normal society.

The veneer of normality was important also in relation to economic problems. The North's economy, built on the three pillars of shipbuilding, linen, and agriculture, had declined drastically in the postwar period. The Unionist government's belated response was to offer major incentives to foreign industrialists to set up production in Northern Ireland. This was coupled with a regional strategy of abandoning Belfast, with its aging infrastructure, in favor of provincial towns as the site for incoming industry. The effect of this was to speed up the process of urban decline in Belfast.

The British approach to economic decline in Northern Ireland after 1972 differed in a number of ways from that of the unionists. First, there was an increase in the incentives offered to foreign industrialists. Second, Labour direct rulers in particular believed that economic revival would lead to political progress. These two tendencies came to the fore under Roy Mason, Secretary of State for Northern Ireland from 1976 to 1979. Central to Mason's faith in the political effects of economic intervention was his concern with image. He was the first Secretary of State to travel widely, particularly in the United States, praising the Northern Ireland economy. These trips were considered a counterbalance to the daily news footage of bombs, shooting, death, and destruction. Mason's vision was apparently shared by two other Ministers in his direct rule team, Don Concannon and Ray Carter. The concern with image thus pervaded numerous aspects of government policy. One example is highly relevant here. From the early 1970s, there had been a major program of urban redevelopment in Belfast that caused large areas of urban

blight. One such area was Sailortown, at the end of the M2, the motorway that linked Belfast to its airport and the main shipping port at Larne. At a time when exresidents of Sailortown were demanding new houses to replace their demolished ones, the Northern Ireland Office was engaged in a major landscaping scheme at the end of the motorway, using land that could not be used subsequently for housing. Concannon was questioned about this in a television interview, and in his reply managed to encapsulate the Northern Ireland Office's concern with image. He stressed that foreign industrialists arriving by sea and air entered Belfast on the M2, and their first view of the city was of urban blight. Landscaping was necessary, he said, because first impressions were lasting ones.

Concannon was responsible for overseeing a campaign in 1976 titled "Operation Spruce-Up." David Speir, on behalf of the Art College, cooperated with Concannon and Belfast City Council in obtaining two murals as part of this campaign. Both were abstract murals, painted on boards by art students Libby McLaughlin and Joan Clarke, and later hung outdoors. Clarke's mural was displayed prominently, perhaps not coincidentally, in Corporation Street at the end of the M2. Pleased with what he saw, Department of the Environment Minister Carter decided to expand the scheme in the following year into a major community murals operation.

History does not record if a single hardheaded American or German industrialist was persuaded to invest in Northern Ireland after seeing an abstract mural at the end of the motorway. Nevertheless, Belfast's brief encounter with community murals was about to begin.

THE BEGINNING OF THE COMMUNITY MURALS PROGRAM

Northern Ireland Office money for the mural scheme was channelled through Belfast City Council's Community Services Department. The Department, in conjunction with the Northern Ireland Office's Department of the Environment, the Arts Council, and the Art College, provided representatives for the committee in charge of administering the scheme. David Speir represented the Art College, and the Department of

Community Services was represented by its Director Dorita Field.

Despite the enthusiasm of the Department of the Environment for the spruce-up campaign and of David Speir for "bringing art to the people," the first year of the community murals scheme was significant for the caution with which the committee proceeded. Perhaps most cautious was the Community Services Depart-

ment. City managers are not normally ac-
customed to dealing with artists. In addition, the
Department was only in its second year of existence and was very carefully attempting to feel
its way.

One of the first moves of British politicians
after the beginning of the "troubles" was the
"relegation" of local government (Tomlinson
1980). Accusations of sectarian bias had been
central to civil rights agitation. Thus the British
transferred responsibility for health, education,
and welfare to nonelected Boards, and the councils were left with few powers.

When a community development program
took place in the North it did so totally outside of
local councils. The British established a semi-
autonomous body, the Northern Ireland Community Relations Commission, which lasted
from 1969 to 1974 (Rolston 1980). The closure of
the Community Relations Commission provided
the Northern Ireland Office with a chance to
continue some program of community development and to bolster up local councils at the same
time. Unionist politicians had not been happy
with the loss of power involved in the relegation
of local councils, yet there was no way the British
were going to return responsibility for health,
education, or welfare to the councils. Community development seemed a perfect solution;
it could placate unionist councilors by giving
them more responsibility, and at the same time
not involve them in allocating resources in any
areas that were political minefields from the British point of view. Thus, local councils were permitted from 1976 on to establish Community
Services Departments with power to build and
run community and resource centers and to hire
staff to deal with community groups.[4] At about
the same time councils were given responsibility
for another "harmless" area of administration—
leisure services—one that became a veritable
growth industry in Belfast particularly in the late
1970s. Given all this, Belfast's Community Services Department was treading very carefully in
1977. There was concern to avoid public controversy, especially if it could be construed as sectarian.

Notices went up in the Art College offering
students paid employment during their summer
vacation—£40 per week for eight weeks. Any

student might have been expected to have
jumped at the offer. But there was more than
opportunism involved: here was a chance not
merely to make money but also to be paid for
pursuing one's vocation. It seemed too good to
be true, as Yvonne McCullough recalls.

> The students were very excited about it . . . they
> thought at that time it was a chance to show the
> people what they could do themselves. . . . I re-
> member thinking: "Oh, it would be lovely to see
> my paintings on a twelve foot gable end wall"—
> which, of course, was nonsense, but that's what we
> thought.[5]

The students, admittedly in a more naive way,
were replicating David Speir's notion that the
scheme involved them in bringing their art to the
people. Their first shock was to discover that the
Committee demanded that their murals could
only be initiated after consultation with groups
in the communities where they were to work.
Yvonne McCullough recalls

> We were specifically told: "You can't just walk into
> areas and do your own thing." Then we began to
> realize we would be actually acting as tools for the
> City Council or for the people in the community
> . . . We had to do exactly what they wanted.

For students being trained to be highly individu-
alistic artists, such a restriction was a major one,
as Yvonne McCullough concludes:

> It was difficult because, obviously, when you've
> been through an arts college training and you sud-
> denly find yourself in a community area, you want
> to talk about your ideas, which are far away from
> the ideas of the community.

Interestingly, only two of the art students employed during the five years of the scheme, Ray
McCullough and Ernie Francis, were graphic de-
signers rather than fine art students. In the process of being trained as artists who undertake
commissions for a fee and thus having to please
the client, they do not seem to have encountered
the same initial reality shock as the fine art students. For most of the students, however, the
stipulation about liaising with the community
was the first sign that this was not to be sponsorship without strings.

There were other obstacles on the path to a
completed mural. In addition to coming up with

an idea for a local mural in consultation with local groups, the artists then had to "sell" that idea to the Committee at City Hall. At this stage they had one further instruction to guide them; the Committee told them not to paint anything political. The students were going to be working in areas in which there were strong paramilitary groups. The Committee presumably feared that the barb in the tail of urging consultation would be that politically naive students would be dealing with politically aware groups in ghetto areas and thus would become pawns in the production of propaganda.

If this was a fear, there was little chance of it being realized. By the late 1970s, Belfast's once strong community movement had passed its peak. There were many reasons for this, not least the effect of government policy in coopting the movement. The community development officers of the Community Relations Commission and the community services officers of the local councils strove to deal with "properly constituted" community groups and, as time went on, mainly with community groups providing a service in their local areas. By 1977, if there were

other organized groups in the community with different, more radical, or far-reaching intentions, they frequently fell outside the orbit of the Community Services Department, especially in relation to receiving council funding. In such a case there might be a plurality of groups in a local area, but only a few would have the blessing of the City Hall as being properly constituted and respectable. These were the groups the Department contacted to ask if they wished to participate in the community murals scheme.

If the community groups responded cautiously, it was more out of ignorance than opposition. Belfast never had had a community arts scheme. In addition, it can be assumed that many of the respectable community groups were far from keen on being swamped, as they would have seen it, by a horde of art students splashing paint all over their community centers. Certainly, the caution was not caused by any politically articulated fear of being coopted by the local state; by design, the local state considered the groups through which the community murals scheme was channelled to be respectable.

COMMUNITY MURALS, 1977–1981

By the end of the summer of 1977, seven murals were completed. The reaction in local areas was mostly positive. The sense of the mural as collective property spread beyond the community group immediately involved, to the point where the mural became a badge of local identity, "an outward emblem of local community pride" (Loftus 1980a, p. 8). This was most obvious in the case of the Woodvale mural in which Ray McCullough and Ernie Francis reproduced a photograph of five local children on a full gable wall. McCullough recalls that the depiction of local children gave the mural an immediacy for the community that made it very popular. In addition, there was much media coverage of this mural, and, unlike much of the news about working-class areas such as Woodvale, it was not about death and destruction.

The local people were happy that something positive was coming out of their area, something they could be proud of.

Not all the murals were equally popular at

local level. In Springhill, Brendan Ellis and Geraldine Jordan painted a mural 400 feet long and ten feet high in an astonishing two-and-a-half-week period. Although this stood as a re-

Springhill Avenue, 1977. Jungle scene. Artists: Brendan Ellis and Geraldine Jordan. (Courtesy: Belfast City Council, Community Services Department.)

Springhill Avenue, 1977. Jungle scene. Artists: Brendan Ellis and Geraldine Jordan. (Courtesy: Belfast City Council, Community Services Department.)

cord of almost demonic artistic genius, the content annoyed many locals. It depicted a jungle with animals and human figures painted with a ferocity that derived as much from the speed of painting as from Ellis's fascination with German expressionism. Local people regarded it as an insulting comment on them and their area, as Des Wilson (1983, p. 19), a community priest resident only a few yards from the mural, explains.

> With brilliant and astounding absence of sensitivity, the artists painted a series of wild animals set in a jungle. Then they went away leaving the residents to contemplate their handiwork and to wonder if it really represented the artists' view of them and their district. Local children soon made amendations to the design, a series of additions, subtractions and appendages to the animals which caused the more elderly and sedate to look the other way. The mural may have been an outsider's comment on the district; the amendations were the children's comment on the artists.

Ellis and Jordan had not consulted with the community as required by the Committee. The local involvement was confined to a couple of teenagers helping the artists. In this sense, the artists did merely bring their art to the people, and the people were not pleased. One wonders what would have happened if consultation had occurred; would the theme have been a jungle?

Would the imagery have been so savage? The suspicion must be that the artistic fury of Ellis could not have been tamed easily by a community group in the same way that, for example, Briege Ryan and Yvonne Mulholland (later McCullough) suppressed their own artistic desires to paint to order for their community group. They worked closely with the community group in deriving both the theme and design of the mural. Like Ellis and Jordan's mural, theirs had flora and fauna, but it was much smoother and softer. Although they clearly wished not to paint "a surrogate landscape to make up for the total lack of greenery in the area," the overall effect of their mural on a dead end street in the New Lodge area was on an incongruous, sentimental image. The presumption must be that the artists were capable of more innovative and imaginative work, but their artistic ability was subordinated to the desires of the local group.

The extent to which Ryan and Mulholland went to involve the local group probably represents the limit of consultation. It is interesting that they still ended up questioning the exact meaning of involving the community.

> . . . the term "community arts" is something of a misnomer since the mural, and the relatively short time we had to do it, worked against involving the community. . . . The children were involved in the painting of the mural and were enthusiastic about

Ashton Street, 1977. Flora and fauna. Artists: Briege Ryan and Yvonne Mulholland. (Courtesy: Belfast City Council, Community Services Department.)

it, but the feeling was that they were helping us with something we were doing instead of the other way round.

This conclusion accurately pinpoints the problems involved in operationalizing the notion of consultation. First, the term *community* is extremely nebulous; even if one confines one's definition to "the community group which asked to have a mural," there are still problems in involving local people. In that first year consultation in planning the theme ranged from nil to full, but community involvement in transferring that design to a wall was partial. It entailed only local children or teenagers who helped to paint parts of the mural.

In retrospect, it appears that although some level of consultation was necessary to concede a certain legitimacy to a mural, there was no direct relationship between the level of consultation and the extent of the mural's acceptability. The overall acceptability of a mural seems to have depended on a complex and ultimately unquantifiable bundle of factors, including not only the level of consultation, but also the theme, the style, the credibility of the community group itself, and the personalities of the artists. For example, Philip McConnell painted an abstract landscape on the outside of the community center in Ainsworth Avenue, and local people destroyed the mural shortly afterwards. Opinion is divided as to whether rejection derived from the abstract style or because McConnell and the community group members did not get along well. On the other hand, the mural of Ray McCullough and Ernie Francis in Woodvale was incredibly popular, not because of the level of local people's involvement—which was negligible—but because it depicted five local children.

By the end of that first summer there seemed no doubt on anyone's part in relation to community murals. The Community Services Department was convinced that the mural scheme had a future; the art students were clear that mural painting was a financially and artistically rewarding way to spend a summer; and community groups knew that, at their best, murals were a source of community solidarity and an object of, for once, positive media attention. Thus, when the scheme was revived in the summer of 1978, community groups scrambled to

have a mural in their area. The Committee went through the same processes as the previous summer, and eighteen murals were completed that second summer.

Despite a wide range of themes in the 1978 murals, it is clear from reading the artists' reports to the City Council that they were inspired by a few underlying motives. For example, a strong expression of anti-urbanism runs throughout a number of murals. In Short Strand, John Coyle and Dave Scott painted a jungle scene on the walls of St. Matthew's primary school playground. It was much less ferocious than the jungle painted by Brendan Ellis and Geraldine Jordan in Springhill the previous year. Scott and Coyle noted that "the theme of the mural was suggested by the local representatives, chiefly Sister Gemma, and we accepted." But one still wonders where the propensity for jungle scenes comes from. It is not confined to murals in Northern Ireland. Cooper and Sargent's (1979, pp. 24, 45, 47) overall survey of murals in the United Kingdom contains photographs of jungle murals in Manchester, Dundee, and Newcastle-upon-Tyne. Many mural artists in Belfast knew about this book, and perhaps its popularity influenced their willingness to chose jungle scenes or to accept that choice when made by others. Perhaps, though, there was something more fundamental at stake. In 1977 Ellis and Jordan had written

> After several meetings and discussions with the teenagers, one of them came up with the idea that as they all lived in a "concrete jungle" would it not be good to at least make it a proper jungle with all the colour and imagination it could contain?

Moreover, we have already noted David Speir's concern with the alienation of modern life and his use of the same term "jungle" in relation to housing estates.

A less forceful anti-urbanism also may be at the root of another tendency, that of portraying rural scenes in the midst of built-up areas. In 1978 alone, Gerald Devlin and Geraldine Cousins painted a country railway station on the wall of a community center in Tyndale, Elizabeth McLaughlin and Jacinta Duff painted another country scene in the Bone area, and Briege Ryan and Avril Lyons, returned again to the theme of flora and fauna in the Silverstream area. There is quite a coincidence involved here, especially in the case of Ryan and Lyons. We have seen already the extent to which Ryan and Mulholland went in 1977 to involve the community in planning the theme of the mural. Given that consultation was with different local people in 1978, how did Ryan and Lyons arrive at such a similar theme? They note that in Silverstream, although "the choice of theme was the result of consultation . . . our brief was fairly open—we were asked to do something bright and acceptable to all the users of the centre." Perhaps Ryan's experience of success the previous year overdetermined her interpretation of such an unspecific brief. Or perhaps there was an unconscious process of judgment afoot. Because romanticism has deep roots in Western culture and art, much of the anti-urbanism of the murals may have derived from the artists themselves rather than from local people, despite consultation.

Such romanticism did not necessarily lead only to aversion from urban themes and escape into rural idyll. Many students delighted in being accepted in the working class areas in which they were working. For some of them, there were barriers of class and religion to be crossed for the first time while painting a mural. The experience could be exhilarating, but it also could be one which was assimilated by them solely at the level of condescension. John Clarke and Virginia Doloughan, painters of a bright circus scene, noted:

> Throughout our stay at Torr Heath we have got to know its people . . . We can recognize their habits and ways of living. Women cleaning and sweeping, Mr. Cochrane walking his dog to the shops. . . .

Although not the only source of inspiration, such "slumming" could be at the base of the choice of theme for a mural. Despite that, the end product could well be judged by local people as a celebration of their urban area. Nowhere was this more true than in murals that depicted actual local people or scenes. In 1978, John Waies and Leonard McCann painted a mural in the St. James area showing people sitting on a bench. They noted that their mural, although only partially complete, emerged unscathed from a vio-

Donegall Road, 1978. Local people on park bench. Artists: John Waies and Leonard McCann. (Courtesy: Belfast City Council, Community Services Department.)

Herbert Street, 1978. Footballers. Artists: Lynda McDonald, Philomena McKeown and Ann O'Rawe. (Courtesy: Belfast City Council, Community Services Department.)

lent period in the area in early August—a sign, they took it, of the mural's acceptability to local people. In Herbert Street, Lynda McDonald, Philomena McKeown, and Ann O'Rawe painted local footballers; this mural also was very popular with local people. Likewise in Highfield, Billy Taggart, chairperson of the local community association, praised the mural painted by Derek Seymour and Terry Murphy, which depicted local kids in boxing gloves. Taggart saw it as a turning point for an estate plagued by vandalism.

Highfield, 1978. Boxers. Artists: Derek Seymour and Terry Murphy. (Courtesy: Belfast City Council, Community Services Department.)

Woodvale, 1978. Local pensioners. Artists: Ernie Francis and Raymond McCullough. (Courtesy: Belfast City Council, Community Services Department.)

Most others were to be pictures of flowers, cartoon characters, things like that. However, we plumped for a picture of our boxers: something to start the identity process, something in which everyone in the estate could take pride and feel part of. And since the picture was painted, it hasn't been touched. (*Belfast Newsletter*, 9 November 1978)

Finally, in Woodvale, Ernie Francis and Raymond McCullough,

decided to continue our idea of using local characters as a theme for the mural and we believed that two old-age pensioners would be suitable as a subject.

The final product, again, was a photographic-style mural of two well-known women in the area.

It is easy to criticize such murals and their artists, as Loftus (1980a, p. 10) does.

> The sporting scenes, though closely related to local club activities, are depicted in the painting-by-numbers style also used for most of the murals of local people. This seems to have been devised by graphic students, keener on deadlines than the elusive perfection pursued by their fine art counterparts.

But this misses the extent to which local people identified with such murals. Although they had no opportunity to be involved in the artistic process, except perhaps in discussing the theme, helping with the painting in minor ways, and generally supporting the artists, local people genuinely identified closely with murals that depicted local people, activities, and scenes. This identity meant that they had a close relationship with the murals; such murals were "theirs" in a way that even the most excellently executed fine art mural was not.

This point can be illustrated by comparing the Ainsworth and Roden Street murals, both painted in 1978. In Ainsworth, John Carson and Maureen Davis painted a mural that profoundly affected local people. Taking the cover of a "Ladybird" children's book on shipbuilding as their source, they painted a scene of welders in Harland and Wolff shipyard. Artistically the mural fitted the wall perfectly, incorporating windows in the wall as skylights in the mural. Local people could easily identify with it because local men traditionally worked as welders in the shipyard. Moreover, it fitted well with the two nearby murals of Francis and McCullough. Together the three murals in the Woodvale area formed, as Watson (1983, p. 8) puts it, "a sort of three ages of man"—children in Disraeli Street, working men in Ainsworth Avenue, and pensioners in Montreal Street. The measure of the Ainsworth mural's success is, paradoxically, that it was carefully destroyed by local people. The welders were painted out with the same shade of

blue as predominated in the mural. This oblitera-
tion was highly politicized, a protest of some
local people about unemployment. A long tradition of being welders in the shipyard had been
broken, and there was no room for depicting the
past when the present was so bleak.

The mural by John Cooney and Cathal Caldwell in Roden Street did not suffer the same
highly politicized fate as that of the welders, but
this was a sign of its political irrelevance to local
people. It is, as Loftus (1980a, p. 10) describes it,
a "breathtakingly flamboyant" painting of a sort
of cosmic skateboarder. The source, an advertisement in a skateboard magazine, was as mun-
dane as that for the welders' mural, but the style
was totally different. Cooney and Caldwell
turned the skateboarder into a surrealistic
character, like Icarus soaring toward the sun on
wheels as well as wings. The end result was
spectacular, but the content and style had little
social or political relationship to the new houses
in the Roden Street estate. The mural was one to
be admired from a distance, like the skateboarder himself, for artistry and skill, but it reflected nothing of the local people to themselves.

This element of reflection, perhaps more than
any other, accounts for the distinction between
identification and mere admiration. Yet it was
somehow an intangible element. There was no
advance guarantee that a mural would be acceptable to local people. In Dee Street, Leslie Nicholl
and R. McNeice did not get on well with the
community group, although their mural's theme
was shipyard workers. Concerning the Tudor
Street mural, Camilla Brown and Seamus Carmichael noted that "the theme was left in our
hands." Taking a cue from the street's name,
they portrayed Henry VIII and some of his wives
in what was a competent enough mural. It was
not one, however, about which the whole community was totally ecstatic.

Eighteen murals in one summer was a major
accomplishment, and barring some doubts and
disagreements, the community groups were
pleased overall with the murals. The artists, for
the most part, were also pleased, despite com-
plaints about too much bureaucracy—"too much
talk and not enough paint," as Fergal Ellis and
Brian Sproule put it. Liam McCauley and Jimmy
Phillips also complained about "the red tape at

*Tudor Street, 1978. King Henry VIII and wives. Art-
ists: Camilla Brown and Seamus Carmichael. (Courtesy: Belfast City Council, Community Services
Department.)*

*Lord Street, 1979. Spiderman. Artists: Leslie Nicholl
and Rhonda Brown.*

Tennent Street, 1980. Jack and the Beanstalk. Artists: Winnie Garrity and Peter McCann. (Courtesy: Belfast City Council, Community Services Department.)

the 'Big Green Dome'," that is, City Hall. But the Community Services Department at City Hall was pleased with the operation of the scheme. Despite some trouble with cautious community groups and, as some Community Services officials saw them, cantankerous artists, the scheme was now working smoothly: only two years old, it was now operating as a matter of routine.

Seven murals were painted in 1979 and another seven in 1980. Themes from fairy tales and children's entertainment abounded. For example, Leslie Nicholl and Rhonda Brown painted Spiderman in Lord Street in 1979, and in the same year, Joan Clarke and another student painted a scene from Snow White on the Save the Children Fund hut in the Lower Oldpark. The next year Winnie Garritty and Peter McCann painted Jack and the Beanstalk on a gable wall in Tennent Street; Andre Stitt and Brian Cunninghan painted dragons in a play area in Unity Flats, and Trevor McIlnea and Rhonda Brown portrayed the Muppets indoors in Ava children's ward in Belfast City Hospital.

For the most part, the only local people closely involved in the murals in the first two years were young people. This trend continued in 1979 and 1980. For example, the Teddy Boys theme painted by Bridget Lindsay and Maureen Connolly in Springmartin in 1980 was chosen by

teenagers in the youth club, on whose walls the mural was painted. Moreover, community artists frequently became surrogate youth workers, giving art lessons on rainy days, organizing competitions, and directing young people who were helping with the painting. This aspect alone could be enough to explain the tendency toward fairy tales, circuses, and children's stories. On the other hand, it is likely that a major element in choosing some of these themes came from the artists themselves, intent on giving the young people what they thought young people would want and like.

This would help explain the strange absence of political content in the murals. There are no flags, sectarian slogans, paramilitaries or protesters, British army, police, helicopters, or guns. This absence is heightened when considering a series of murals done by primary school children in the 1970s under the supervision of artist Neil Shawcross[6]; among the children's drawings of universal houses, trees, and buses there are frequent recognizable scenes of Belfast, including the large crane, Goliath, at Harland and Wolff shipyard, and British army helicopters in the sky.

If primary school children can depict day-to-day aspects of a familiar war, why not politicized teenagers? The answer must be, at least partially, that they were not encouraged to do so. This was easy enough, given that in most cases the young people were only marginally involved in choosing the theme. But more importantly, there was an actual veto on political content in the murals.

That veto at its most formal level derived from the Committee at City Hall. One aspect of their early caution that never disappeared was their determination that they could not be charged with sponsoring offensive murals. However, the story of the state-sponsored murals does not involve highly politicized communities and artists being thwarted in their attempts to have political murals. First, few of the murals had any political content, deliberate or otherwise. The only two that had any both date from the first year, 1977.

In North Queen Street, on the wall of a recreation hall, Cathal Caldwell and Ethel McLaughlin painted a scene from *Gulliver's Travels*. In it, an emperor makes his ministers jump over a line parallel with the horizon. The artists said they

North Queen Street, 1977. Gulliver's Travels. Artists: Cathal Caldwell and Ethel McLaughlin. (Courtesy: Belfast City Council, Community Services Department.)

would "localise" the story by painting the line orange and the emperor green. The allusion was fairly obscure, and was meant to be.

> . . . the people responded pretty well to it. They'd come up and say: "Well, I know what that really means." And we would nod our heads and say: "Yes, it's your view" and so on and so forth; but really, you know, it could fit into any view.

Perhaps not as obscure was that they had the green emperor shaking his fist across the open ground in front of the recreation hall toward the local police barracks/army post. It is said that the police and army protested at the fist; but it merely may be that some of the more aware members of the City Hall Committee realized that some political statement may have been construed. Either way, the Committee ordered Caldwell and McLaughlin to mute the political point by having the emperor's fist clasp the orange line rather than gesture defiantly across the open space.

In the same year, Tom Nevin and Fergal Ellis painted Humpty Dumpty on the wall of the community center in Newhill. When the mural was finished, some local people felt that Humpty Dumpty looked amazingly like Secretary of State Roy Mason. Nevin has claimed that any similarity was totally accidental, but, be that as it may, the political joke had been made and the

City Hall Committee was unable to do anything about it.

The Committee did change other murals. For example, the 1980 mural of Jack and the Beanstalk, painted by Winnie Garritty and Peter McCann, originally had the giant holding a knife, ready to cut down the beanstalk Jack was climbing. On paper it may have looked fine, but in reality the forty-foot-high giant brandishing a large dagger faced the playground of a primary school. The headmistress objected to the violence depicted, and the Committee had the artists change the knife to a stick.

Dorita Field, then Director of Community Services, seems to have been the prime mover in such situations. In 1978 Ray McCullough and Ernie Francis had included the words "Woodvale Housing Association" in part of their mural of pensioners, and Field had it removed in case it gave the impression that the Association had paid for the mural. On other occasions she was even more idiosyncratic. Deirdre Mullan and Angela McMacken, working on a mural in the Sunshine Club, included a sun, to which Field inexplicably took exception. On another occasion, she wanted bees included in a mural, although the artists did not. Some artists were annoyed at this, but not all. Yvonne McCullough resented Fields's interference because "I felt I was responsible for putting that mural on the wall and I wanted to feel totally responsible for my

Newhill, 1977. Humpty Dumpty. Artists: Tom Nevin and Fergal Ellis. (Courtesy: Belfast City Council, Community Services Department.)

mural." Her husband Ray, the graphic designer, was more pragmatic: "The person who holds the purse strings can call the play. They were paying, they had the power."

But even if the committee censored little, censorship was occurring all the same. Yvonne Mc-Cullough puts it this way:

> Local people might want a flag or tank or soldier in the mural, and we would have to say: "No, we have been told, nothing political . . . so lets think of something else." It stopped with us. It was censured with us. It didn't get as far as the City Hall.

Ray added:

> I expect if it had been something quite strongly political, it wouldn't have got through. It would have been weakened down at the very least. But it didn't arise with any of us.

Donegall Road, 1981. Local street scene. Artists: Colin McGookin and Dermot Delargy.

Loftus (1980a, p. 9) backs up this experience of two artists by noting that a number of the artists she spoke with

> voiced their admiration of the political use of wall-paintings in America but felt that by attempting something similar in Northern Ireland they would be caught by the old sectarian pitfalls . . .

This avoidance of politics was one sign of the routine that was already established by 1979. Watson (1983, p. 3) notes another sign, that "the later murals often have a predictable atmosphere about them which reeks of the factory line." This may be one reason why local community groups ceased clamoring for murals; perhaps they had seen enough fairy tales, jungles, and circuses in other areas to know they had no desire for the

Donegall Road, 1981. Local street scene. Artists: Colin McGookin and Dermot Delargy.

Donegall Road, 1981. Local street scene. Artists: Colin McGookin and Dermot Delargy.

vignette of local community life. The artists were Colin McGookin and Dermot Delargy. The same year saw a nostalgic mural in Divis Flats depicting the area as it was before the high-rise flats were built. But such interesting work notwithstanding, it was clear the scheme had run its course. Labour had been replaced by the Conservatives and Northern Ireland, which unlike Britain had not experienced any major cuts under Labour, began to feel the edge of Tory cuts. The murals were not expensive—about £1,000 each—but they also were not a priority of a Department of the Environment under a monetarist cabinet. The City Council seems to have had its fill of administering the scheme, and the new Director, Brendan Henry, was less enthusiastic than the now-retired Dorita Field. In the

same in their own. Consequently, as the summer of 1981 approached, it was clear there were no applications for murals from any community groups. The Community Services Department responded in a twofold manner: first, diverting some funds into sculpture and community photography (only one sculpture was erected, but it was dismantled soon afterwards because of insurance problems); and second, frantically trying to persuade community groups to take a mural team.

Four areas were persuaded, and among them the St. James area ended up with nine small murals in the bricked-up windows of a disused factory (now a supermarket), each mural being a

Divis Flats, 1981. Local street scene.

Arts College, David Speir also was about to retire.

Most important, the community groups were no longer enthusiastic, as Ray McCullough concludes: "Most of the areas that wanted murals had murals and there weren't that many new areas around." Of course, artists could have been employed to maintain the murals, but, given the declining interest of City Hall, this only happened superficially; Tony O'Neill was employed for one summer to look after all the murals. Consequently, as Watson (1983, p. 3) states, the murals "have swiftly become budding eyesores, irrespective of their original artistic value." Thus there was not much left other than nostalgia, as John Waies and Leonard McCann foresaw as early as 1978.

> Ultimately, of course, through time the colours will fade, but for many years to come in this community I think people will look at it and say: "D'you remember the summer the artists painted a mural for us?"

CONCLUSION

In many areas touched by the Council-sponsored community mural program, only a memory remains. The ravages of weather and urban redevelopment have obliterated most of the murals and sometimes even the walls on which they existed. By the late 1980s, the only murals to remain in any recognizable shape were those (mentioned earlier) in the blocked-up windows of a disused factory, simply because they were protected by the security fence erected around the building when it was converted into a supermarket.

This does not mean there were no community murals after the City Council scheme ended. In the mid to late 1980s in particular, a number of community murals appeared. Some were sponsored by a local community group or youth club. A grander scheme to "brighten up Belfast" organized by Bryson House, a large voluntary work agency, and paid for by the Belfast Action Team, a government-funded initiative for the inner city, led to a dozen or more murals in 1987–1988.[7] Many of the murals of this period were poorly executed, and most returned to the famil-

Artillery Youth Club, North Queen Street. Spray can art. Artists: Anthony Lynn and Keith Connolly.

iar "community" themes—children, nursery rhyme or cartoon characters, and scenes of rural bliss in the midst of urban decay. The harvest scene in Springhill Avenue, the grazing cows in Upper Meadow Street, and the rolling hills painted on a corrugated iron "peace line" at Berwick Road draw attention to the poor environmental conditions of the present by their very incongruity.

Some of the murals, particularly in the New Lodge area, stand out on the grounds both of relative professionalism and originality. A collage-type mural painted in 1987 by young people on a wall of Artillery Youth Club was bright and eye-catching in the manner of the American spray-can street art on which it was based. A 1988 mural nearby in Upper Meadow Street was similar to a number painted during the state-sponsored community mural program in that it showed people involved in sport; unlike in these earlier murals, however, the sports represented were Gaelic ones, football and hurling.

The state-sponsored mural scheme ended in 1981, never to be revived. There is no direct link between the community murals of the late 1970s and those of the late 1980s.

There is a final point to be considered in relation to lasting effects. Some of the artists involved in the Council program point to what they see as an indirect effect of that program; namely, that there was an *explosion* of political mural painting in Belfast in the summer of 1981. Yvonne McCullough points specifically to one aspect of this link—an art student who worked on the council murals, complained about their lack of politics, and later found his niche painting openly political Republican murals. More generally, Ray McCullough is equally emphatic on the direct link involved.

> Graffiti was the message on the wall before the (state-sponsored) murals came along. You had the written word on the walls. Then when the (political) murals came along came the visual image. I don't think it's just a coincidence. I think that the fact that we were producing the (state-sponsored) murals before that, people could see the impact; they turned from the written word to the visual image.

This assessment is faulty on several counts. Yvonne McCullough's example notwithstanding, there is little evidence of a link at the personnel level between the council murals and the later political murals. In addition, the political mural explosion, when it came, was not confined to Belfast, but occurred almost simultaneously in Derry, Armagh, Newry, Lurgan, and elsewhere, that is, in many areas that had never seen state-sponsored murals. Moreover, the Belfast scheme had been carefully spread across the sectarian divide to both nationalist and unionist working-class areas; yet the political mural explosion of 1981–1982 was confined to nationalist working-class areas. Thus it seems farfetched to see a close link between both sets of murals.

The state-sponsored community murals did not change the world; they did not stop urban blight; they did not end the "troubles," and they did not even survive as symbols of community identity in the long term. But these facts can only be judged as failures if one expected them to fulfill any of these monumental conditions. The Council murals were partly about environmental improvement in areas suffering from urban blight and the ravages of urban guerrilla conflict, partly about convincing some people that government had a caring side, partly about legitimizing both the newly established Community Services Department of Belfast City Council and some respectable community groups, partly about giving local kids something to do during the summers, and partly about an ingenious way to use art students as surrogate youth workers. In all these ways, the Council mural scheme was at least temporarily successful. However, it neither encouraged nor quelled any political upsurge in local areas. As mentioned at the beginning of this chapter, the "cooling out" of the local community in Northern Ireland was a task taken on by larger political forces than an experimental community mural scheme, and the explosion of Republican murals in 1981 was ample proof that that "cooling out" process had had little success.

3

Art as a Weapon: Republican Murals

THE SURVIVAL OF NATIONALIST IDENTITY

Despite centuries of colonialism—which included the decimation of its population through famine, the decline of its language and social system, and the subordination of its economic and political systems—there is a strong sense of cultural identity in Ireland. Folk memory has turned oppression into a badge of identity, just as the oppression itself gave rise to numerous forms of opposition. Thus, the seventeenth-century penal laws (which forbade the Irish to inherit land, hold public office, carry a weapon, or own a valuable horse), Cromwell (who presented the native Irish with the choice of hell or the barren wastes of Connacht), and the famine (which halved the population of Ireland within a few short years) are powerful memories and symbols to this day. But as remembered events they symbolize not merely the cruelty and tragedy of oppression, but also the possibility of opposition. Even in the darkest days of the penal laws, native children were taught ancient Greek and Latin in "hedge-row" schools, and hardly a generation went by without some sort of military response to foreign rule. In short, because of the historical experience of oppression, there is a strong sense of cultural identity in Ireland.

But that identity has not been shared equally by all the people of Ireland. Particularly in the last two centuries, the equation has been established in many minds that to be Irish is to be Catholic. This derives not merely from the fact that the planters who colonized parts of Ireland in the seventeenth century were Presbyterian and Anglican, but also from the fact that an early attempt at a cross-sectarian political alliance failed miserably. The United Irishmen of 1798 represented a shaky alliance of forces: on the one hand, landless Catholic peasants, and on the other, Presbyterian businessmen and professionals inspired by the republican ideals of the French Revolution to oppose English economic and political dominance in Ireland by force. The Act of Union of 1801 was supposedly a stick to punish the Presbyterian middle class for its rebellion, but it also became a carrot to entice that class to change its sense of identity in a remarkably short period of time. After that point, Irish nationalism and Catholicism became increasingly intertwined and indistinguishable.

This led to a certain amount of historical revisionism in nationalist consciousness. The penal laws, for example, came to be remembered as religious oppression, although they also were economic and cultural. The image that summed

69

up the penal laws in the popular mind was of the hunted priest saying mass on a rock for a bedraggled congregation, some of whom kept watch for approaching soldiers. Other images were theoretically possible—for example, the economic image of the impoverished landless peasant family—but within the equation of nationalism and Catholicism, it was the religious image that more often prevailed.

The equation has also allowed for interpreting not only past events but also current ones, in a religious or quasi-religious manner. Thus Patrick Pearse, leader of the 1916 Rising, believed that the spilling of blood had a cleansing, sanctifying effect.[1] In a similar vein, the 1981 hunger strike can be presented in overwhelmingly religious terms, as a human self-sacrifice similar to that of Christ (Collins 1986). This aspect of nationalist consciousness and symbolism is easily open to criticism. Some commentators (for example, Kearney 1978) have seen an unbroken line from the mythology of Pearse (part Christian, part pre-Christian) to the contemporary IRA. The latter is said to be motivated less by political ideology than by "theology" (Berman, Lalor, and Torode 1983). Such criticisms miss the mark in many ways, however. For a start, religion played a part in the survival of cultural identity, and distasteful as that may seem to the enlightened academic mind, it is not so in the popular mind. But perhaps more significantly, the criticism misses the extent to which consciousness and identity represent a complex mixing of elements, both religious and secular. Nationalism is not a unitary ideology, and the extent to which the religious mode predominates differs from time to time, as well as between different forces within the nationalist camp. It is not merely that religious images can be reinterpreted in secular terms (Christ as a victim of Roman imperialism, for example), or vice versa (for example, the notion that the establishment of democratic socialism in Ireland will involve "a reign of social justice based on Christian principles"—Sinn Féin 1970, p. 3), but that nationalist popular consciousness involves a complex interweaving of both secular and religious elements. This is evident in the nationalist minority in the North.

When Ireland was partitioned in 1921, Northern nationalists became reluctant citizens of the new state of Northern Ireland. At its strongest, this reluctance was evidenced by an IRA campaign against the new state and the refusal of some nationalist-controlled local councils to cooperate with the new government. In addition, nationalist teachers refused to accept salaries from the new Ministry of Education and instead were paid by the Free State government. For them, at least, the existence of the Northern state was a temporary affair. But the millenarian fervor passed, the IRA campaign faded, the councils were replaced by commissions, and the teachers were paid by the Northern government. Nationalists settled down to a more or less sullen acceptance of the political fait accompli. Nationalist politicians were elected to the Northern parliament, but did not take their seats until 1925; it was 1965 before the Nationalist Party accepted the official title of parliamentary opposition. The nationalist professional middle class came to terms with its position on the edges of unionist privilege, mostly confined to servicing the needs of the nationalist working class. And the nationalist working class was confined geographically, politically, and culturally in its own clearly defined ghettoes.

It might be thought that the alienation of nationalists from the Northern state represented a proverbial chicken-and-egg riddle: did they opt out, or were they excluded? The answer depends on the politics of the person answering. But one fundamental point is obvious: although sectarian division already existed in the North, it was institutionalized and thereby strengthened as a result of partition. Nationalists in the North had been relegated historically to specific geographical ghettoes. There were separate school systems for Catholic and Protestant children, and nationalists had their own forms of dancing, music, and sport; and, although threatened, the Irish language continued to survive. All of these cultural forms had experienced a major revival in the latter years of the nineteenth century with the formation of organizations such as the Gaelic League and the Gaelic Athletic Association. Although these organizations had middle-class leadership, their effect on popular culture was profound, demonstrated by the spread of the cultural practices they encouraged. Apart from various other intangible cultural differences, these practices clearly distinguished the nationalist population from the unionist one, even before partition.

Partition cemented the differences. Within the Northern state, the two cultures were clearly ranked in a hierarchy with unionism at the top. In a situation where nationalists were subordinate economically, politically, and culturally, they clung to whatever identity they had even more tenaciously than they might have done in a more egalitarian situation. Gaelic sports became widespread. At various points, especially in the thirties and forties, folk dancing (ceili dancing, as opposed to the more formal dancing for competitions) became mass entertainment. The Irish language experienced less mass support, but it never died, kept alive at least in formal education in the still-separate Catholic schools.

All of this cultural expression went on without impinging much on the daily lives of unionists. The existence of the two separate cultural worlds was such that few unionists knew the extent to which these cultural practices existed in the nationalist community. Given its nature as a subordinate and oppositionalist culture, nationalist culture had little or no outlet through formal state channels of communication; what did pass was often "laundered" to suit more refined middle-class unionist tastes.[2] In addition, some of the cultural practices—such as flying the Irish tricolor—were forbidden by the state. Finally, the bulk of cultural practices was safely hidden away in the ghetto, confined to parochial halls, schools, and playing fields. Thus with unionist culture dominant, nationalist culture was relegated to the margins of unionist society.

These cultural practices became essential to nationalist life, not merely as a pastime or hobby, but as a badge of identity in the face of unionist dominance. Whether every nationalist realized it clearly or not, partition ensured the increased politicization of nationalist culture in the North.[3]

Given this, it is perhaps surprising that there was little of the popular visual arts element in this strong nationalist culture. This is not to say that there were not traditional visual symbols available for nationalists. The harp, for example, dates back at least to the time of Henry VIII, circa 1534. Usually it appeared on coins or banners with a crown over it. As Hayes-McCoy (1979, p.

23) concludes, linking symbolism to politics,

> We may speak of the Irish struggle of modern times as one to remove the crown from above the harp and to place the harp itself on a green field instead of a blue.

The unencumbered harp also appeared as a symbol of a free Ireland in the musical tradition. Thomas Moore's popular song "The Minstrel Boy" has the minstrel destroying the strings of his harp after being captured in battle.

> Thy songs were meant for the pure and free,
> They shall never sound in slavery.[4]

Another traditional symbol was the phoenix, the mythical bird that was reborn from its own ashes. Used originally in Ireland by the Fenians in the late nineteenth century, it signified for them the continuation of the republican struggle in their generation despite the failure of the revolutionaries of the previous generation, the Young Irelanders. It eventually came to have similar significance for subsequent generations, each taking up the struggle despite the defeats of those who went before them.

The association of green with Ireland has been mentioned already, but in 1830, with the Young Ireland Movement, it was linked with orange and white to form the tricolor. With the emergence of republicanism in Western Europe, tricolors had been developed as the national flags of several countries. The Young Irelanders' choice of colors for their tricolor was not random: green symbolized celtic Ireland, orange the planter tradition, and white union or peace between the two (Hayes-McCoy 1979, pp. 140–143).

But beyond their limited use in flags or printed publications, neither these nor any other symbols found much expression in the North after partition. There was no popular tradition of visual representation of nationalist symbols and historic events. Most noticeably, there was no working-class tradition of mural painting such as existed at the time in unionist areas. The most that occurred was the emergence of a minor tradition of banner painting in the Ancient Order of Hibernians (AOH), a conservative and mainly rural nationalist organization. Like the organization as a whole, the banners of the AOH almost slavishly imitated those of the Orange Order. The themes were different, but the style was identical. AOH members wore and still wear sashes that are green instead of orange.

The explanation of this absence can only be speculative. Loftus (1980a, p. 5) has suggested that pictorial representation on the nationalist side was diverted into religious art. But such art was sponsored by institutional church and bourgeois interests to be consumed by worshippers of all classes. There was little popular equivalent of the custom, as existed in Mediterranean Catholic countries, of believers producing their own paintings and statues for use in processions and celebrations. Moreover, there was no cross-fertilization of imagery, as seen in working class Mexican-American mural painting, in which Our Lady of Guadalupe is both a Catholic and a national symbol. Although there was religious art on the nationalist side, it was not popularly produced (although popularly consumed) and was confined basically to the religious, rather than directly political, domain.

Of more importance in explaining the absence of a popular pictorial tradition in nationalist culture is that opportunities for public display of nationalist symbols were severely restricted, both by law and unionist state practice. The 1954 Flags and Emblems Act forbade flying the tricolor in situations in which it could cause a breach of the peace. In practice, the RUC interpreted any display of the flag as provocative, no matter how hidden from unionist gaze. The Union Jack, on the other hand, as the national flag was not included in this legislation and could never in practice be judged as provocative by the security forces of the unionist state, whatever the intentions of those displaying it. Similarly, mural painting was a legitimate and respectable tradition in unionist areas; but nationalists in general and republicans in particular could not expect to escape unscathed if caught by the RUC painting nationalist symbols or slogans on their walls. Thus the relationship of nationalists to the Northern state helps explain the absence of popular pictorial cultural forms. Nationalist culture was expressed in several confined forms, such as dancing, music, and sport. These were confined not least in the sense that, with the exception of sport, they took place in-

doors. Even in the ghetto, the streets and walls were policed by the unionist state.

Moreover, many of the traditional symbols, such as the harp and tricolor, were claimed by both constitutional nationalists and militant republicans in the North. Once the state became established, the republican movement declined. In 1927, as one old member recalls, a meeting was held in Belfast to attempt to revive the almost moribund movement.

> All of Sinn Féin was there, Cumann na mBan, the Army, the Fianna were all there, and out of the whole lot there wasn't forty people. (quoted in Munck and Rolston, 1987, p. 167)

Despite sporadic campaigns in the North between the twenties and the sixties, community support for republicans and their military action was marginal. Constitutional nationalists, however, gained credibility in the nationalist community not least because of their larger-than-life leader for the first thirteen years of the Northern state, Joe Devlin. Although they recognized the legitimacy of the state in practice, they still had the support of many, including some more militant nationalists who might vote for them for tactical reasons, that is, to prevent a unionist candidate winning. In such a situation, the constitutionalist nationalists' claim to the use of tra-

Ardoyne, 1953. Mural to commemorate 150th anniversary of rebellion of Robert Emmet. (Courtesy: Daniel Wasson.)

Lenadoon Avenue, 1980. "Don't be a fireside Republican."

ditional nationalist symbols was accepted. Thus although they had the legitimacy, middle-class nationalists for the most part did not have the inclination or access to paint symbols on working-class walls. Republicans, on the other hand, despite having more access to working-class walls, had less opportunity to paint on them, given the clandestine nature of their struggle. The streets policed by the unionist state were not fertile ground for oppositionalist art, particularly militant republican art.

Republican messages on walls were confined to slogans, often hastily scrawled. But a more general nationalist message did manage to make its way to the walls in mural form on at least one occasion, the 150th anniversary of the rebellion of Robert Emmet in 1803. In Ardoyne[5] the streets were decorated with bunting and a mural was painted. On one side was a harp, and on the other a bust of Emmet. Both were surrounded by a frieze of laurels and underneath were the slogans: "Robert Emmet Commemoration" and "Erin go Bragh" (wrongly spelt "Eirn go Bragh," that is, "Ireland forever"). Although some republicans may have been on the committee behind the celebrations, the overall thrust of the mural was not republican, and it was painted without state interference, and survived, although very faded, until redevelopment in the area twenty years later.

Even the escalation of political conflict in the North from the late sixties on did not lead to a

nationalist mural movement. At most some of the slogans became more ornate, such as the one "Join your local unit of the Irish Republican Army, Oglaigh na h-Eireann, in the fight for freedom" (a photograph appears in Breslin 1972, p. 67). Eight years later a similar message appeared in Lenadoon: "Don't be a fireside republican, be a fighting one." As the conflict continued, certain walls became strategic ones for these more ornate slogans. One, on a corner of the Falls Road, the main artery through nationalist West Belfast, carried the following slogans within three years, each replacing the one before: "700 years is too much" (alluding to a 1976 Northern Ireland Office poster campaign against political violence that read: "Seven years is enough")[6]; "Will Lizzie visit H Block?" (coinciding with the Queen's visit to the North in 1977); and "Stonemason will not break us" (referring to Roy Mason, Secretary of State from 1976 to 1979).

Occasionally the slogans became almost mural-like. One was the slogan on the wall of the People's Garage in Andersonstown in the mid-1970s, which referred to political prisoners: "Until all are free, we are all imprisoned" (photograph in Collins 1983, p. 186). But there were few nationalist murals before 1981. One exception for which photographic evidence exists is a mural of the bust of the 1916 revolutionary

Hopefield Street, early 1970s. Portrait of James Connolly, Irish tricolor, and Starry Plough flag.

leader James Connolly, painted on a wall in Hopefield Street, Ardoyne, in the early 1970s. This was the period after the split between the avowedly Marxist Official republican movement and the initially narrowly nationalist Provisional republican movement. Because Connolly was originally adopted by the Officials as a political exemplar, this mural was probably painted by people in or close to the Official republican movement. In Derry in the mid-1970s, Provisional republican supporters painted an unarmed IRA volunteer standing to attention as part of the annual Easter celebrations of the 1916 Rising.[7]

Westland Street, Derry. IRA volunteer.

PRISONS AND CULTURAL REVIVAL

The emergence of a popular political art form on the nationalist side can be traced back to the imprisoning of republican activists and sympathizers that began with the introduction of internment in August 1971. Approximately 300 nationalists were interned without trial (McGuffin 1973). Like republican internees for generations before them, they had numerous collective ways in which to survive the indeterminacy and hardship of internment. In the compounds (or cages) of Long Kesh and Magilligan internment camps or on the prison ship *Maidstone*, they derived their own command structure and rules. In addition, they began to develop ways of collective self-education in such areas as Irish history, politics, and language. Later, when phasing out the compounds, Lord Gardiner gave as one of his reasons that "there is virtually a total loss of control by the prison authorities inside the compounds."[8]

Of particular interest as a form of collective solidarity and survival was the internees' discovery of political art.[9] Wood carving, painting, and leather work were popular, and numerous artifacts—carved wooden harps, painted handkerchiefs and wooden plaques, and leather purses and handbags—began to emerge from the internment camps into the homes of relatives and friends in the nationalist community. Celtic

designs predominated, particularly in the wood and leather work. The themes of the paintings ranged from traditional nationalist symbols, through copies of Che Guevara posters, to depictions of republican struggle. Apart from the harp and the tricolor, the celtic cross and the phoenix were common symbols in the paintings.

Some of the internees discovered a talent for such work that surprised not merely fellow internees, but also, given their total lack of art training, the artists themselves. The less talented had tracings to copy from, but multiple use of such tracings caused problems, as Bobby Devlin (1985, p. 13) recalls.

> One of the first items I made was a plaque with one of the leaders of the 1916 Rising, Patrick Pearse's profile painted on it. This was sketched on from a well-worn tracing, and Pearse's nose was badly out of shape. As I was not a perfectionist, I finished it and proudly sent it out . . . when it was being passed through the searching point, a screw . . . remarked on how unusual it was to see a plaque with an image of Brian London, the boxer, on it.

Other aspects of Irish culture flourished within the internment camps, especially music and the Irish language. But the art work, even at its worst, was the most visible aspect of the cultural revival. The internees were developing a cultural form which—unlike the music and the language—did not then have an equivalent in the wider nationalist community, and they were producing it on such a scale that eventually a large proportion of working class nationalist homes gave pride of place to their very own Long Kesh harp, plaque, or framed painted handkerchief.

In 1972, in the first attempt to phase out internment, juryless courts (called Diplock courts after the British judge who recommended their introduction) were inaugurated. But people sentenced in them still received political status and were imprisoned in the compounds with their political command structures; they were not classified as ordinary criminals. By 1976, however, the compounds were phased out on the recommendation of Lord Gardiner, and all subsequently sentenced prisoners were treated as "ordinary criminals."[10] This "criminalization" policy was met with sustained opposition from republican prisoners.

Between the ending of internment and criminalization, the solidarity of the prisoners expressed itself in a continued heightened political and cultural awareness. Young prisoners educated themselves in political theory and science, and their later emergence into leadership roles in the republican movement shifted the movement noticeably to the left in the late 1970s. Culturally, the Irish language became immensely important to the prisoners. Admittedly it was a strange Irish, almost an argot of its own; as one life-sentence prisoner's wife (Rolston and Tomlinson 1986, p. 179) put it: "it's their Irish; I don't think it's an Irish anyone else could understand"—but it was a potent symbol of their collective identity. Because Irish-speaking areas are referred to by the term *Gaeltacht*, in time it was possible to quip that Long Kesh was a "Jailtacht." In addition, speaking Irish was a form of communicating without the screws being able to understand.[11]

The cultural artifacts that flowed from the jails into the communities not only reminded people that the prisoners were still alive and should not be forgotten, but they also were propaganda for the movement. The flow of artifacts dried up

with the blanket protest beginning in 1976. Republicans refused to wear the prison uniform, as this would be a symbol of their acceptance of the label "criminal." Instead, they wore only prison-issue blankets. Eventually prison officers refused to allow them out to the toilet without prison uniform, and so the prisoners spread their excrement on the walls to dispose of it. Alone in the cells of the new hyper-modern H Blocks, they were allowed no books, pens, or paper. But they found ways of smuggling articles in and began writing letters (called "comms," short for communications) that were smuggled out later. These illegal letters told the story of the H Block protest to the outside world. In addition, the blanket prisoners continued painstakingly to teach each other the Irish language.

> It was great the way I was able to learn Irish. You stand at a cell door, maybe with the lead of a pencil, and a man who has Irish shouts out a word. Maybe he was one of the men who learned it in the cages. Anyhow, you write down the word and the phonetic spelling beside it, and the meaning, and then you repeat it. That goes on all day. if you haven't a lead, you can use your Rosary beads" (blanketman Joseph Maguire, quoted in Coogan 1980, p. 4).

In a similar way, news (referred to by the Irish word *sceal*), songs, history lessons, even potted versions of popular novels were communicated between the isolated prisoners. As Maguire recalls, "one man, Bobby Sands, memorised 'Trinity' by Leon Uris. That took eight days to tell."[12]

Later, Sands became famous as the first of a group of ten republican prisoners to die on hunger strike demanding the reinstatement of political status. His face became widely known, not merely because of the daily appearance of his picture on TV news broadcasts, but also because of the emergence of a wave of murals in nationalist areas. Sands's face and words were prominent in these murals. Perhaps this way, more than any other, made the link between community and prison clear.

THE HUNGER STRIKE AND THE FIRST
MURALS

The hunger strike came at the end of an esca-
lating contest of wills between the authorities
and the protesting prisoners that occurred during a four-year period. Finally, in October 1980, a
hunger strike of republican prisoners was called.
It ended two months later based on apparent
concessions from the British government. But
when these concessions were not forthcoming, a
second hunger strike began in March 1981. Unlike the first, when seven men began together
(later joined by three women from Armagh Jail),
the second hunger strike was staggered. It began
with one man only, Bobby Sands, officer com-
manding the H Block republican prisoners.
Sands was followed periodically by other prisoners until, after the deaths of ten strikers, the
prisoners called off the hunger strike.[13]

During the four years of build-up to the hunger strike, the issue of the prisoners' blanket
protest was kept alive by a small number of support groups consisting primarily of relatives of
protesting prisoners, the Relatives' Action Committees. They marched, held conferences, gave
numerous media interviews, and picketted officials at home and abroad, often clad only in
blankets, like their prisoner relatives. Initially
they worked in a vacuum, but by the time of the
hunger strike, much valuable propaganda had
been disseminated because of the prisoners' per-
sistence.

In the nationalist communities in particular,
this propaganda raised popular awareness about
the protest. For example, one of the most popular songs sung by folk groups in drinking clubs
in nationalist areas was "The H Block Song."
Written by Dungiven singer Francis Brolly about
his younger brother who was on the blanket, it
tells how a young man became a protesting prisoner. Moved by injustice, he fought back; when
captured he refused to accept the label "criminal," as the chorus of the song puts it:

> I'll wear no convict's uniform
> Nor meekly serve my time,
> That Britain might brand Ireland's fight
> Eight hundred years of crime.

Such folk songs were a practical medium of
communicating a political message. Escalation of
the war in the 1970s resulted in increased support for republicanism and the expression of that
support at several levels, including music. There
were numerous folk groups that did the rounds
of the drinking clubs with their republican
songs. At times there was a veritable republican
hit parade, with new songs commemorating the
latest daring escapade available on record within
days of the event. But overall there were contemporary songs that quickly became established as
favorites, such as "The Men Behind the Wire"
and "Four Green Fields," alongside the old reli-
able republican anthems such as "On the One
Road" and "A Nation Once Again." Brolly's "H
Block Song" fitted easily into the genre and
quickly became popular.

As the prison crisis grew, there also occurred a
proliferation of slogan writing on nationalist
walls, "Smash H Block" being the most common.
These slogans were scrawled by nationalist
youths sympathetic to the prisoners' protest not
least because, with as many as five hundred prisoners on the blanket at any one time, there were
few nationalist youths who did not have a relative or friend protesting in prison.

With the second hunger strike, organization of
propaganda and solidarity work became the task
of the local H Blocks and Armagh Committees.
Their actions included white line protests (standing along the lane markings of main roads holding pictures and names of hunger strikers),
pickets, and eventually public fasts, where
makeshift shelters were erected, signatures to
petitions collected, and large display boards revealed clearly to passers-by the number of days
each hunger striker had been fasting.

Among the first to be highly active in this
propaganda and solidarity work were young
people. This had much to do with the perceived
character of the first hunger striker, Bobby
Sands. At 27, he was still a young man; yet, like
many youths from nationalist areas, he had
spent a number of years in prison: from 1973 to
April 1976, and from October 1976 until his
death in May 1981. Thus he was someone with
whom working class nationalist youths could

easily identify, experienced as they were in police and army harassment and frequent arrest for "screening" purposes.[14] In addition, Sands had been elected a Member of the British Parliament for Fermanagh/South Tyrone only one month before his death. His profile was high in the mass media throughout the hunger strike. But the media had only one photograph of Sands they could use. With his long hair and friendly smile, he appeared a normal, personable character, not the monster that the Northern Ireland Office would have had people believe he was. At one point during the hunger strike, BBC chiefs in London requested a less engaging photograph of Sands from the Northern Ireland Office, but none was available (Curtis 1984, p. 204). Finally, Sands revealed himself as an able and emotive writer with his poems and descriptions of daily life in prison. These had been published from 1978 on in the weekly republican newspaper *An Phoblacht/Republican News* under the pen name "Majella" (his sister's name). Halfway through his hunger strike, ten pieces were republished by Sinn Féin in a best-selling pamphlet (Sands 1981). Of these, one of the most popular was "The Lark and the Freedom Fighter," an allegorical story in which the analogy is drawn between the lark's torture and eventual death at the hands of its captor and Sands's own situation.

In nationalist areas, numerous youth support groups were formed. Some were more or less independent, and others were aligned closely with the local H Blocks and Armagh Committee. All sought ways to be politically active on behalf of the hunger strikers. Like their elders, the young people marched, picketed, and so on, but they also covered the walls with graffiti calling for political status or the smashing of H Block. Also common was reference to the five demands of the hunger strikers: no prison uniform, no prison work, free association, education facilities, and full remission. As the situation became more desperate with the imminent death of Sands, increasing care was taken in drawing the slogans. Walls were first painted over with white or black paint and the slogans carefully painted in large black or white letters. In a sense, the slogans became almost mural-like. These quasi-murals seem to have emerged first in the Lenadoon area. Some were in Irish; for example, one

Lenadoon Avenue, 1981. "Tiocfaidh an lá nuair beidh Éire saoir aris" ("The day will come when Ireland will be free again").

Lenadoon Avenue, 1981. Excerpt from "A Letter to a British Soldier on Irish Soil."

used a phrase that had emerged from the Irish-speaking blanketmen themselves: "Tiochfaid Ár Lá" ("Our Day Will Come"—see Sands 1983, pp. 59–60). Most were in English, such as the one containing lines from Patrick Galvin's poem "Letter to a British Soldier on Irish Soil":

When you came to this land,
You said you came to understand.
Soldier, we're tired of your understanding,
Tired of British troops on our soil,
Tired of the knock on the door,
Tired of the rifle-butt on the head,
Tired of the jails and the beatings,
Tired of the death of old friends,
Tired of the tears and funerals,
Those endless, endless funerals.
Is this your understanding?

From an early stage there was symbolic representation in the quasi-murals—the *H* of H Block, the Starry Plough,[15] the tricolor, and the Fianna flag.[16] Even before Sands's death, paintings of black coffins emblazoned with white crosses also appeared.

One other artistic propaganda tactic was to use existing commercial advertising hoardings, but to tamper with them to have them portray a republican message. Thus, on the Falls Road an advertisement for Bass, showing a man raising his glass in a hearty toast, had the slogan "Great stuff this Bass"; it was simple to substitute "IRA" for "Bass."

In a sense it was a short step from the quasi-murals and the hoardings to the first actual murals that appeared a few miles away from Lenadoon in the Ballymurphy estate. On a gable wall a black background was painted. Over this, with a few simple strokes, were painted the busts of two blanketmen and alongside them were the words of the chorus of "The H Block Song." Around the corner from this mural, a large commercial advertising hoarding was blacked out; painted over it in white was a simple portrait of a blanketman, the letters *H* and *A* (for Armagh), the names of the first four hunger strikers, and the slogan, "Victory to the

Whiterock Road, 1981. Blanketmen and words of chorus of "The H Block Song."

Springfield Road, 1981. Blanketman, tricolors, and names of first four hunger strikers.

blanketmen POW" (prisoners of war). This mural also contained two small tricolors, providing the only dash of color. The vintage of these murals is revealed both by their simplicity of style, including the straightforward monochrome approach, and because they precede the death of Sands. The clenched fist mural, for example, does not mention the hunger strike.

THE MURAL EXPLOSION: THEMES AND SOURCES

After Sands's death, an explosion of murals occurred in nationalist areas. Within a few months, at least one hundred were painted in Belfast, fifty in Derry, and others in nationalist areas of Armagh, Lurgan, Newry, and Strabane. The emotional tension of the times is clear not merely from the content of the murals but also from their quantity. In terms of color, complexity, and quantity, nationalist areas had never witnessed anything like this before.

Given that the hunger strike was the immediate cause of the mural explosion, it is not surprising that the strike was their most common theme. The theme was most commonly portrayed by depicting a hunger striker, real or figurative. Of the hunger strikers, the one portrayed most frequently was Sands.

The photograph of the smiling Sands that had caused problems for the BBC was reproduced in painted form in several places, accompanied frequently by some text or slogan. Thus, the electronic media ironically played its part in disseminating an image that was central to oppositional propaganda. On the side of a supermarket on Shaws Road, a small picture was accompanied by a slogan in large letters: "The Right Honourable Bobby Sands Esq MP, murdered by his fellow members of HM government." The word "murdered" was emphasized by being painted red, thus countering a common argument from some British politicians and church leaders, as well as the Northern Ireland Office, that Sands's death was suicide. In a mural

Creggan Heights, Derry, 1981. Portrait of Bobby Sands; "The Spirit of Freedom."

Oakman Street, 1981. Portrait of Bobby Sands, skeletons, and slogan.

Shaws Road, 1981. Portrait of Bobby Sands, excerpt from his "The Spirit of Freedom," and slogans.

in the Creggan, Derry, the accompanying words were simply a phrase from Sands's writings: "The spirit of freedom." In Ardoyne the smiling Sands was included in a well-executed mural that looked like a high contrast photograph. Also included was a stylized image of the walls of Long Kesh and the slogan "You cannot put a rope around the neck of an idea." In Beechmount, the bust of Sands was one of several images, including skeletons, one of which was crucified. The source for this mural—surprising perhaps given its highly Christian allusion—was an Iranian poster of solidarity with the hunger strike. But the mural artists added their own element to the overall message with the accompanying inscription:

> The Irish Republican Army is right. The British government does not listen to the ballot box in Ireland and the only thing they will listen to in Ireland is what they listened to in other colonies, agitation, rebellion and armed forces.

Sands was not the only hunger striker to be honored in murals. Near his parents' home in Andersonstown, for example, Kieran Doherty was commemorated. In Derry's Bogside, the heads of all the dead hunger strikers appeared together. There also was a tricolor and a Starry Plough, the latter a flag more closely associated with the Irish National Liberation Army (INLA), three of whose members (Patsy O'Hara, Kevin Lynch and Mickey Devine) were among the dead. In Gobnascale, also in Derry, busts of each of the hunger strikers were painted on walls between the windows of low-rise flats.

Frequently, however, the central figure of a mural was not any specific person, but a figurative blanketman or hunger striker. A common depiction was one drawn from the determination of the prison protesters not to be criminalized— the blanketman as defiant. Thus, in the Creg-

Creggan Heights, Derry, 1981. The conveyor belt of justice.

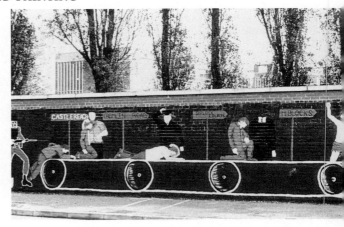

Beechmount Avenue, 1981. The conveyor belt of justice.

gan, Derry, a series of four scenes, painted on boards, shows a man being arrested by the British Army, beaten by the RUC, sentenced by a Diplock court judge, and still refusing to submit; despite what republicans referred to as this "conveyor belt of justice," he ends up on the blanket, without the ultimate symbol of criminal status, the prison uniform. The conveyor belt of justice is treated more explicitly in a Beechmount mural. A British soldier forces a man onto the assembly line belt; he is beaten in Castlereagh Interrogation Centre, held on lengthy remand in Crumlin Road Jail, sentenced in a Diplock court, and finally is depicted on the blanket in Long Kesh prison. The notion of defiance is also caught in other ways, as in the Falls Road mural in which a sturdy *H*, constructed of bricks, is broken by a blanketman rising off his knees. Continuing the allusion, the slogan reads "Break Thatcher's back."

Considering the injustice of the system, as well as the severe beatings blanketmen received frequently when they refused to conform, it was possible to portray them as victims rather than rebels. Thus on Finaghy Road North, a blanketman is on his hands and knees, his blanket around his waist. The notion of passive suffering is also caught by one of the slogans: "Lord, may their sacrifice like yours not be in vain." In Ardoyne, an identical kneeling blanketman, although this time with his blanket around his knees, is accompanied by a slogan demanding faith as a central component of solidarity with those suffering: "For those who believe, no ex-

Beechmount Avenue, 1982. "PLO-IRA: One Struggle."

Beechmount Avenue, 1988. Mural in solidarity with African National Congress.

Beechmount Avenue, 1982. Portrait of James Connolly, signatory of 1916 Proclamation of Independence.

Chamberlain Street, Derry, 1985. Celtic figures and symbols, and words of Padraic Pearse's poem "Mise Éire."

I Scuimhne agus in onóir

VOL. JOSEPH COYLE 1970	VOL. ETHEL LYNCH 1974
VOL. THOMAS McCOOL 1970	VOL. JOHN McDAID 1974
VOL. THOMAS CARLIN 1970	VOL. JAMES MOYNE 1975
VOL. EAMONN LAFFERTY 1971	VOL. BRIAN COYLE 1976
VOL. JAMES O'HAGAN 1971	VOL. DENIS HEANEY 1978
FIANNA GERRY DONAGHEY 1972	VOL. PATSY DUFFY 1978
VOL. COLM KEENAN 1972	VOL. GEORGE McBREARTY 1981
VOL. EUGENE McGILLAN 1972	VOL. CHARLES MAGUIRE 1981
VOL. JOHN STARRS 1972	VOL. EAMMON BRADLEY 1982
VOL. SEAMUS BRADLEY 1972	VOL. PHILLIP O'DONNELL 1982
VOL. MICHAEL QUIGLEY 1972	VOL. RICHARD QUIGLEY 1984
VOL. JAMES CARR 1972	VOL. DANNY DOHERTY 1984
VOL. JOHN BRADY 1972	VOL. WILLIAM FLEMING 1984
VOL. JAMES McDAID 1972	VOL. CIARAN FLEMING 1984
VOL. JOSEPH WALKER 1973	VOL. CHARLES ENGLISH 1985
VOL. GERARD CRAIG 1974	
VOL. DAVID RUSSELL 1974	
VOL. MICHAEL MEENAN 1974	

Rossville Street, Derry, 1985. Roll of honor to local dead republicans.

"Comms" (communications) from Long Kesh pr (Above) aspects of republican struggle, and (be British, repression and republican resistance.

Beechmount Avenue, 1987. "Armed Struggle, Pe Politics."

Derry. "There can be no British solution in Ireland."
(On boards; artist: Joe Coyle.)

Cable Street, Derry, 1984. Aspects of republican
struggle and quotation from Bobby Sands. (Courtesy:
Elaine Thomas.)

Springhill Avenue, 1987. Memorial to eight IRA men
killed by Special Air Services of British army in
Loughgall, County Armagh. (Artist: Gerard Kelly.)

Springhill Avenue, 1987. King Nuada, mythological
character. (Artist: Gerard Kelly.)

Falls Road, 1988. Memorial to three IRA volunteers killed in Gibraltar. (Artist: Gerard Kelly.)

Falls Road, 1988. Birthday greetings to Nelson Mandela. (Artist: Gerard Kelly.)

Monagh Road, 1988. The dying Cuchulain, and busts of seven signatories of the 1916 Proclamation of Independence. (Artist: Gerard Kelly.)

Cable Street, Derry, 1988. Bobby Sands and Che Guevara.

Etna Drive, 1981. Blanketman.

Falls Road, 1981. Busts of blanketmen, names of hunger strikers, and crucifix over H Blocks. (Courtesy: Paddy Hillyard.)

planation is necessary; for those who don't believe, no explanation is possible."

Clearly there was religious symbolism in a number of the murals. Many aspects of the blanket protest and the hunger strike lent themselves easily to religious interpretation—the patient suffering of the prisoners; their Christ-like appearance, bearded and clad in blankets; and so on. The religious message could be conveyed by using an unreferenced biblical quotation, as in one Bogside mural: "No greater love hath a man than he lays down his life for his friends." But frequently the reference was more direct, conveyed not merely using words but also using pictorial images. Another mural in the Bogside shows a crucifix and contains the words "St. Peter, let these men enter heaven for they have served their time in hell." In Ballymurphy, a hunger striker lies dying below a hovering angel. An armed IRA man is genuflecting reverentially, whether toward the hunger striker or the angel is not clear. "Their hunger, their pain, our struggle" reads a slogan, and on the scroll carried by the angel are the words "Blessed are those who hunger for justice." The same words from Christ's Sermon on the Mount appear half a mile away on a Rockmount Street mural. Along with them is the image of a dying hunger striker, rosary beads in hand, and hovering over his bed is the Blessed Virgin, bathing him in heavenly light. A few yards away the busts of two Christ-like hunger strikers flank a middle section of a triptych that borrows liberally from Dali's Christ

Donegall Road, 1981. Dead hunger striker being carried from Long Kesh.

of Saint John of the Cross; the crucifix in this instance is suspended over a large *H*. A few yards in the opposite direction is a Pieta-like image. A woman watches as a man carries the body of her dead hunger striker son from Long Kesh. In Beechmount, only a few hundred yards further on, a massive Sacred Heart gazes from above on the blanketman alone in his cell.

Despite the proliferation of religious images in this geographical area, it is interesting that religion does not appear to have been the major influence on the images produced. Secular im-

Beechmount Drive, 1981. Sacred Heart of Jesus over-looking blanketman.

Amcomri Street, 1981. The lark in barbed wire and excerpt from writings of Bobby Sands.

ages were in the majority. As such, these convey defiance rather than simple passive suffering. They relate more easily to the portrayal of the hunger striker as rebel rather than victim. Thus a Beechmount mural shows hands tied by barbed wire; the hands are not limp but are clenched into fists, symbolizing resistance to injustice. The same notion is conveyed using the much used symbol of the lark in barbed wire, taken from Sands's writing. The image was used widely; for example, in Amcomri Street it was

Beechmount Street, 1981. Clenched fists in barbed wire, tricolor, and names of seven hunger strikers.

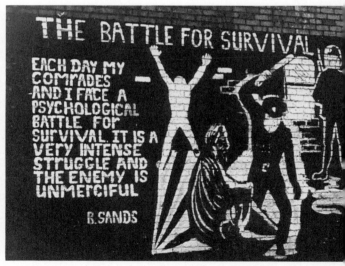

Etna Drive, 1981. Prison officers beating blanketman and excerpt from the writings of Bobby Sands; "The Battle for Survival."

Derrin Pass, 1981. Map of Ireland and excerpt from the writings of Bobby Sands.

Benraw Road, 1981. Celtic cross, IRA volunteer with Fianna flag, and names of hunger strikers.

Juniper Park, 1981. Portrait of Bobby Sands, firing party, and excerpt from Sands's writings.

accompanied by Sands's most quoted statement in the murals:

> We may eventually be murdered. But, dare we say it, similar to our little friend the lark, we have the spirit of freedom that cannot be quenched by even the most horrendous treatment. Of course we can be murdered, but while we remain alive we remain what we are, political prisoners of war.

Words were often as important as pictorial images, whether in the straightforward message in Derry—"We the people fully support the hunger strikers on whatever action they take themselves"—or the numerous quotations from Sands, like that in Ardoyne: "Each day my comrades and I face a psychological battle for sur-

vival. It is a very intense struggle and the enemy is unmerciful"; or that in Derrin Pass, "Everyone, republican or otherwise, has his own part to play."

In this vein, even death is not necessarily the ultimate expression of passive suffering. As the numerous "Final Salute" murals make clear, although these republican activists are dead,

Rockdale Street, 1981. Armed IRA volunteer.

others can take their place, not least those firing the rifles over the coffins. The final salute image was taken directly from a photograph that appeared on the front of *An Phoblacht/Republican News* on 9 May 1981. It showed armed volunteers firing a volley over Sands's coffin. It was copied onto a wall in Twinbrook within yards of his home, accompanied by a quotation from Sands, in Brompton Park, and in a number of other murals.

It is clear from the murals considered to date that, although the hunger strike had the potential to be presented as a solely humanitarian issue, the young mural artists made no attempt to distance themselves from republican armed struggle, happily juxtaposing apparently humanitarian images with more militant ones. Direct representations of republican armed struggle make up the second largest category of the first wave of nationalist murals.

The anonymous volunteer appears in numerous murals. At times he may be holding only a flag, although it is clear that as a volunteer he is prepared to use arms. In Benraw Road he holds a Fianna flag; at Rossville Flats, Derry, it is a Starry Plough. In another Derry mural, the volunteer holding the flag is clearly backed up by armed volunteers in silhouette. More frequently, however he is armed and, although posing for the artist, is nonetheless ready for action. In Andersonstown, the volunteer appears as a figure out of a South American guerrilla group, with his long hair and the slogan "Venceremos." But in Rockdale Street his origins would appear to be more North American; with his close-cropped hair, bull neck, and M-60, he looks like someone from the Green Berets. This latter image, rather than the former, was copied by youths in Derry, as well as the accompanying slogan: "They may kill the revolutionary, but never the revolution." In Lenadoon Avenue he is drawn childishly and does not appear threatening despite the accompanying message:

> Soldier, do you think that you have got away with the murder's of our political prisoner's and innocent children on our street's? Well, think again, for your name is engraved on the freedom-fighter's bullet!

But in Divis Flats he is much more threatening;

Lenadoon Avenue, 1981. IRA man and slogan; "Welcome to Provo Land."

Divis Flats, 1981. Irish National Liberation Army volunteer.

masked and armed, he approaches the onlooker face-on.

On Shaws Road he prepares to fire an RPG rocket launcher; in Derry's Rossville Flats, it is a more old-fashioned rifle. Interestingly, this last mural, depicting a volunteer silhouetted in front of a blazing fire, is based on a photograph of a real incident. During the imposition of internment in 1971, a major gun battle took place between the Official IRA and the British army in the Markets area of Belfast. The Official IRA leader Joe McCann was photographed at a lull in the battle (for the photograph, see Messenger 1985, p. 131), and ten years later the photograph was used as the basis of this mural painted by

Shaws Road, 1981. IRA volunteer with RPG rocket launcher.

Rossville Street, Derry, 1981. Armed volunteer in silhouette.

Provisional IRA supporters. A mural in Rockville Street is also based on a real incident, the killing of 18 paratroopers by the IRA in one incident at Narrow Water, County Down in July 1979. Despite the cinematographic manner in which the incident is depicted in this mural, no photograph exists of the incident, and the depiction derives from the artists' vivid imagination.

Imagination runs totally wild in an Oakman Street mural. In a style reminiscent of a boys' action comic, a British soldier is shot in the neck, and nearby some men hold a tattered Union Jack. The naive approach is evident both in the painting and the attempted poem alongside.

> I lie at night and try to think
> Why our lads in jail are prepared to die.
> The British government sit back and laugh
> But the people know that they are daft.
> Four of our comrades have passed away.
> Is there call for more to die?
> O, British government, use your sights
> And give our lads their five just rights.

Oakman Street, 1981. IRA in action.

Lone Moor Road, Derry, 1981. IRA woman volunteer in action; "Resistance."

Strabane Old Road, Derry, 1981. IRA warning to British army plus British army graffiti in reply.

Rossville Street, Derry, 1981. Cuchulain and roll of honor of local IRA dead.

Benraw Road, 1981. "Out of the Ashes came the Provos."

Divis Flats, 1981. Memorial to republican volunteers, tricolor, and Starry Plough flag.

Lenadoon Walk, 1981. Weapons, flags, and phoenix rising from the flames.

Because it refers to only four dead hunger strikers, this mural is a frozen moment in the struggle that was to take six more lives after the mural was completed.

In all these instances, only male volunteers are depicted. But on at least two occasions, the volunteers of the women's section of the IRA, Cumann na mBan, were celebrated. Sihouettes were used in both. A Rossnareen Avenue mural shows two armed women and the caption "Free our country. Join Cumann na mBan." In Derry, in a mural based on a photograph published in republican magazines, a woman fires a rifle in an act of "Resistance."

Sometimes volunteers were not portrayed at all. On Suffolk Road a rifle and a map of Ireland in green, white and orange stand for the IRA; in one Derry mural, it is an armalite and a tricolor. At Rossville Flats in Derry, the message is spelled out so that no one could miss it; a painting of an armalite is accompanied by the note "A weapon of the Provisionals." An armalite in Andersonstown stood not just for the whole republican movement, but also for the protesting women prisoners in Armagh jail.

Thus with its weapons and volunteers, the whole movement is being celebrated, and in some instances commemorated. In Rossville Flats, beside a painting of the dying mythical hero Cuchulain, there is a roll of honor of the IRA volunteers killed in action in Derry. In Divis Flats two busts painted on a wall reveal that the

mural is a monument to dead INLA volunteers Matt McLarnon and Danny Loughran. Despite the deaths, however, the movement is alive and strong, powerful enough to exercise control over areas. On the main road into Gobnascale in Derry, therefore, an IRA volunteer, painted on an advertising hoarding, stands guard: "Warning! Irish Republican Army occupied territory. British forces enter at own risk," he warns, a message that British soldiers have responded to with graffiti on the same hoarding.

The vitality of the movement is in marked contrast to its near demise in the late 1960s. The year 1969, with the siege of the Bogside in Derry and the loyalist attack on the Falls Road in Belfast, heralded the rebirth of the movement. Thus a number of murals, such as one in Benraw Road, remind us that "out of the ashes that was Belfast came the Provos." The phoenix was a symbol of great importance, representing the reborn republican movement. It is the central symbol in murals in Lenadoon Avenue and in Derry. On Andersonstown Road, alongside some words of the old ballad "A Nation Once Again," it rises from the flames to break an *H* made of brick. In Beechmount Avenue, the phoenix symbolizes not merely the republican movement but the nationalist people as a whole: "The people arose in '69, they will do it again at any time." In one Twinbrook mural, the phoenix reference is oblique; an armed volunteer is rising from the flames. This same mural notes the date of the Easter Rising, 1916, pointing out the continuity of struggle—1916 to 1969 to the present and its hunger strike.

Thus there is a sense of history in the murals. Sometimes this is explicit, as in a poorly executed Twinbrook mural showing the bust of Theobald Wolfe Tone, the late eighteenth-century revolutionary and father of Irish republicanism, together with a quotation from him: "Too long we've borne with smouldering wrath the cursed alien laws." Taking more recent historical figures as a theme, a Rossville Flats mural depicts Pearse and Connolly together. But the historical mural par excellence is the copy on a wall in Beechmount Avenue of Jeff Perks's epic linocut, reminiscent of Picasso's *Guernica*, depicting Ireland as a centuries-old training ground for British repression; it was copied and slightly al-

Rossville Street, Derry, 1981. Portraits of Padraic Pearse and James Connolly, leaders of the 1916 Easter Rebellion.

Beechmount Avenue, 1981. Centuries of British repression in Ireland.

Andersonstown Road, 1981. Militarized Britain striking Ireland; "Sasenach Amach" ("British Out"). (Courtesy: Marilyn and Dave Hyndman.)

Beechmount Avenue, 1981. Four images of British repression in Ireland.

Rossville Street, Derry, 1981. Britain/Thatcher terrorizing Ireland; "Get the Brits Out!"

tered in the process from the original as it appeared on the cover of a pamphlet calling for British withdrawal (Committee for Withdrawal from Ireland 1980). Yet it is noteworthy that this masterpiece with a historical theme was linked to the present by joining it to another less well executed mural. Therefore at the end of a line of British soldiers over centuries repressing the Irish, the final soldier of this mural, a member of the local British regiment (the Ulster Defence Regiment), forces a republican activist onto the conveyor belt of justice depicted in the adjoining mural (referred to above).

History itself, then, was relatively unimportant: even the republican "saints" received little wall space. Instead, history was seen as all the events that led up to the current struggle, but that struggle was by far the focus of the murals—whether it was the armed struggle of the republican movement or the prison struggle of the blanketmen and hunger strikers. Similarly, current repression is a minor theme in the first wave of murals. At Rossville Flats, Derry, one mural simply listed the names of the fourteen people murdered by British paratroopers on Bloody Sunday, 30 January 1972. In Beechmount, a series of four small murals, some of which were copied from postcards produced by Leeds Postcards, laid out repression in general terms. One showed a hand, with Union Jack cufflinks (in the original the cufflinks were pound sterling symbols), squeezing Ireland. The second showed a prisoner behind bars, the bars being in the mouth of a military officer. The third showed someone crucified on a Union Jack, the fourth showed Ireland, Christ-like, carrying a cross. In Andersonstown, a mural using the symbol of the Troops Out Movement in Britain showed a militarized Britain striking a bloody Ireland and urged "Sasenach Amach" ("Brits Out"). In similar terms, a highly original Rossville Flats mural depicted Britain with Thatcher's head, teeth sunk into the North of Ireland, and shaking the whole island furiously.

AFTER THE FIRST WAVE: LATER REPUBLICAN MURALS

Because the trigger for the nationalist murals was the hunger strike, it might be expected that the ending of that strike should have seen the decline of murals in nationalist areas. This was not the case, however. The first fervor was past, and, perhaps consequently, the quantity of murals declined. There was still a respectable number produced, however, particularly in the first year or so after the hunger strike. The reason for this can be traced to the newfound legitimacy of Sinn Féin.

The hunger strike ended in confusion. The British government did not concede the five demands of the prisoners, and the continuing death toll convinced some relatives, encouraged by some Catholic clergy, to pull their sons, husbands, and brothers back from the brink as each one went into a coma before death. The confusion cleared somewhat when it became apparent eventually, without any fanfare or propaganda, that the British had conceded a number of the demands, particularly the right to refuse prison uniform, the ultimate symbol of criminal status. Despite the apparent defeat, Sinn Féin gained a lot from the hunger strike in popular support. People who had never marched before or had not done so since the days of civil rights went on protest marches or attended hunger strikers' funerals: an estimated 120,000 people attended Bobby Sands's funeral. Young people in particular still had much political energy, and now that the H Blocks and Armagh Committees were defunct, a logical place to go was the republican movement, especially Sinn Féin. The party thus had an influx of new members, new vitality, and new ideas.

One of these new ideas was that of electoral intervention and constituency work. Traditionally, republicans had either boycotted elections while Ireland was partitioned or stood only on an abstentionist ticket. As late as April 1981, when Sands was already on hunger strike, Sinn Féin refused to participate in local government elections in the North. Yet a number of candidates sympathetic to the prisoners' demands were elected, and Sands himself was returned as MP for Fermanagh/South Tyrone in a general election only one month before his death. Given all this, the leadership of Sinn Féin acknowledged later that the failure to capitalize on popular support through the electoral process was a major mistake. Rather than boycott elections, they began to stand as principled abstentionist candidates. Five Sinn Féin candidates were elected to the Northern Ireland Assembly in 1982. Sinn Féin President Gerry Adams was elected Westminster MP for West Belfast in 1983 and again in 1987. But the arena where the new electoral strategy made the most impression was in local politics. Sinn Féin opened a network of advice centers, and an army of unemployed young people taught themselves the intricacies of social security law, housing policy, and so on, and became able advice workers. Eventually, when Sinn Féin stood in local council elections but no longer on an abstentionist basis, they took a large share of the nationalist vote from the previously unchallenged constitutionalist nationalist party, the SDLP. By 1984, Sinn Féin had 59 active councilors in the North and was consistently obtaining about 40% of the nationalist vote in elections.

It was partially in the context of elections that murals continued to play a role in nationalist

Bond Street, 1983. Election mural for Sean McKnight; the lark in barbed wire.

Short Strand, 1983. Election mural for Denis Donaldson.

Bond Street, 1983. Election mural; portraits of Bobby Sands and James Connolly.

areas. The symbols and messages were often straightforward and simple. In Beechmount Avenue, a small 1982 mural showed merely a tricolor and a map of Ireland and urged, "Vote Sinn Féin." In the Markets area in the same year, the lark in barbed wire, the symbol used frequently in the hunger strike murals, now became a badge of identity for Sean McKnight's electoral bid. Nearby in Short Strand, an election mural for Denis Donaldson resembled a cinema poster. Much less grand, but more memorable as a slogan, was the message on a wall in Etna Drive, Ardoyne: "Think 32, not 6. Vote Sinn

Féin." Witty as well as memorable was the neat reversal in a mural in Beechmount Avenue in 1983 of the standard establishment argument that Sinn Féin is merely the political wing of the terrorist IRA: "Parliament is the political wing of the British army." Few of these murals and quasi-murals matched the scale or quality of many painted during the hunger strike.

Grander statements were attempted. In the Markets the attempt did not work well. Busts of Connolly and Sands were painted along with the caption, "Vote socialist, vote republican, vote Sinn Féin." But the artist failed to paint Sands well enough, and the attempt was erased. Later another artist managed a variation on the theme of the smiling Sands photograph of 1981, but the style and scale differed noticeably from that of the bust of Connolly. A successful attempt was the ambitious, two-storey election mural painted before Adams's 1983 election in Beechmount Avenue (renamed RPG Avenue). It shows a young, strong, blonde woman peeling back a tricolor to reveal people marching with placards: "Houses," Youth," "Education for all," "Jobs," "Culture," and "Brits out." Apart from the quality, a number of facts are noteworthy about this mural. First, despite the traditional republican elements in the overall message—"Brits out," the tricolor—other elements are not traditional but reveal the newly adopted wider political concerns of the party. Second, the image of the woman is part old and part new. Ireland often has been symbolized as a woman: Mother Ireland, the Old Woman of Bearra, Caithlin Ni Houlihan, Roisin Dubh. The former two are old women, abandoned and betrayed by their sons (as in the traditional poem "Mise Eire" or the more modern song "Four Green Fields"); the latter two are young women, patiently awaiting rescue from their daily sorrow (as in the traditional song "Roisin Dubh"). All are victims, and the image of Ireland as an old woman has perhaps been used more widely. But in this mural not only is it a young Ireland, but she also is strong, confident, and militant. She represents defiance, not passive suffering, and in her youth and confidence perhaps is the perfect symbol for the revived, post–hunger-strike Sinn Féin. Third, as acknowledged at the bottom of the mural, the money for materials was provided by the republican weekly newspaper, *An Phoblacht/ Republican News*. It is evident that the party had faith in murals as education and propaganda, and also that the mural artists, in this instance at least, were very dependent on the party for materials. Thus, although some murals during the hunger strike were painted by independent or semi-independent groups, the post–hunger-strike murals increasingly became party murals. This was not least because a number of the mural artists, because of their political experiences during the hunger strike, had moved into Sinn Féin and became party cultural workers.

Despite this, the murals became clear party propaganda only occasionally, outside of election time. The most obvious example is the 1982 mural on the gable of Sinn Féin's headquarters at Sevastapol Street. It shows two people reading a copy of *An Phoblacht/Republican News*, the "official organ of the republican movement." The paper obviously gives the republican view of the world, and the admonition here to read it is therefore also by extension a warning about the content of the nonrepublican mass newspapers' treatment of the movement. This aspect of propaganda is portrayed in a 1985 mural in the Bogside. A blindfolded broadcaster speaks into a microphone, in an image lifted from posters of the Paris uprising of 1968. The accompanying slogan reads, "Many have eyes but cannot see." Elsewhere the message is more specific, directed at the *Irish News*, the paper most widely read by

Off Cable Street, Derry, 1985. Blindfolded broadcaster; "Many have eyes but cannot see."

northern nationalists. In Belfast's Kashmir Road, the logo of the *Irish News* is mimicked in the layout of a 1983 quasi-mural: "Irish News, Brit news, Bad news."

Rather than denigrating the opposition, more often the murals are putting across the message and boosting morale in areas in which the republican movement is popular. The posthunger strike message is complex, containing the traditional concerns of armed struggle and state repression as well as the newer interests in elections, community politics, and women's rights. But outside of election time, it is obvious that the newer issues have received less space in the murals. The concern with women's issues was reflected in one 1983 quasi-mural in Lenadoon Avenue, the area where it all began. An unacknowledged quotation from James Connolly stated: "The worker is the slave of capitalist society. The female worker is the slave of that slave." But beyond that, there is nothing. Likewise, there are no murals directly relating to the work of many in Sinn Féin after the hunger strike in local and community politics. There are no murals on housing conditions, debt, or poverty. Even in the area of repression, where there have been active campaigns since 1982, there are few murals. The issue of show trials, in which the British state attempted to reclaim the ground from Sinn Féin by putting republicans (and loyalists) in jail for long periods of time on the uncorroborated word of alleged accomplices (*Belfast Bulletin* 11, 1985), merited only a few quasi-murals, such as that in Beechmount Avenue in 1983: "Stop the show trials." A systematic IRA campaign to remove informers from local communities in 1985 warranted a few chilling quasi-murals, but no more. In Beechmount Avenue, one depicted a coffin with a white cross (surprisingly, a symbol used in earlier murals in relation to republican heroes rather than traitors), and the message, "IRA warning. Touting can seriously damage your health."

The issue of repression, particularly the use of plastic bullets to maim and kill (Curtis 1982), received a little more coverage. In one case, a 1981 mural in Linden Street "in memory of those murdered by plastic bullets" was altered. The original showed a soldier aiming a plastic bullet gun, and in the center, a person screaming. At a later date, after Lieutenant-General Pringle lost a leg in an IRA car bomb explosion in London, one leg of the soldier with the plastic bullet gun was replaced with a wooden stump; and, lest the significance of this be lost on the audience, the officer's name was added. In Derry a 1982 mural commemorates one specific plastic bullet victim, an eleven-year-old boy: "They call the killing of Stephen McConomy civil order," adds the caption cynically. Another plastic bullet victim was Sean Downes, killed by the RUC at a republican march in Belfast in August 1984. In the Bogside, Derry, in the following year, a mural depicted an RUC man with a plastic bullet gun, as well as the bust of Downes. There also is the loaded question, "Who next(?)." Finally, breaking out of the theme of nationalists as merely victims, a mural painted in Moira Street argues that repression gives rise to resistance, in this case, youths with a catapult replying to a British soldier with a plastic bullet gun.

These murals notwithstanding, there were a number of issues of repression and campaigns around them that received no attention on the walls—prison conditions in general, strip searching of women in Armagh jail—or only a few hastily scribbled slogans. Thus the post–

Beechmount Avenue, 1986. IRA warning to informers.

Off Cable Street, Derry, 1985. Portrait of Sean Downes, plastic bullet victim.

Moira Street, 1984. Repression, resistance, and quotation from Bobby Sands.

hunger-strike murals are not only more traditional than the overall mood in the party at the time, they also have a minor focus on some of the more traditional concerns to republicans, those relating to repression. Instead, as in the Moira Street mural, the main theme of post–hunger-strike murals was resistance, particularly the armed struggle.

Treatment of this theme included approaches already developed and perfected during the hunger strike murals. Most frequently armed volunteers were shown either posing with guns or using them. In Beechmount Avenue in 1983, a

Springhill Avenue. Tricolor, Fianna flag, and IRA weapons.

Creggan, Derry, 1986. IRA volunteers in action; "Ireland Unfree shall never be at Peace."

Falls Road, 1982. Women's involvement in resistance.

Circular Road, Derry, 1985. Map of Ireland and armed IRA volunteer.

well-executed black and red mural showed three armed volunteers waiting for action; an almost identical mural was produced on the wall of the Bogside Inn in Derry. In Springhill Avenue in the following year, three volunteers brandished their weapons aloft and repeated in English a slogan of the hunger strike period, "Our day will come." In the Creggan area of Derry, two kneeling and armed volunteers of Oglaigh na hEireann (the IRA) were accompanied by the unacknowledged quotation from Patrick Pearse, "Ireland unfree shall never be at peace." Nearby, a 1985 mural shows a green-uniformed volun-

Falls Road, 1983. Armed women from IRA, Palestine Liberation Organization, and South West Africa People's Organization; "Solidarity between women in armed struggle."

Beechmount Avenue, 1982. Cartoon mural.

Beechmount Avenue, 1985. "Stad Maggie Anois!" ("Stop Maggie Now!")

teer running against a white map of Ireland and an overall orange background; no caption is necessary.

Less frequently guns came to stand for the military struggle in the absence of any figures in the mural. This occurred most obviously in the Ballymurphy/Springhill area of Belfast where between 1984 and 1986 three murals appeared with technically accurate representations of various IRA weapons. There was minimal additional information in word or symbol, suggesting that the guns were message enough. These murals almost appeared as giant pages from a munitions dealer's sales catalogue; in other circumstances the politics revealed could have been very different.

Women volunteers appeared in only two murals, both painted in succession on the same gable wall on the Falls Road in the Beechmount area. In 1982, one painted for International Women's Day showed three women, one giving a clenched fist salute, a second with a microphone, and a third bearing arms. The quotation read, "We must grow tough but without losing our tenderness." In 1983 this was replaced by a highly effective mural. Within the confines of a women's symbol five meters in diameter, three women represent the PLO, SWAPO (South West African People's Organization), and Cumann na mBan. Above them is an armalite and below the caption, "Solidarity with women in armed struggle."[17]

Some of the techniques and references in this mural show an originality not present in many of the posthunger strike murals. Originality also appeared in a few other guises. A 1982 mural in Beechmount Avenue delivered the ultimate accolade to Cormac, the resident cartoonist of *An Phoblacht/Republican News*. One of his comic strips, relating to the killing of three soldiers in nearby Cypress Street, was reproduced on a wall. Further up Beechmount Avenue in 1985, an original idea was used: a map of Ireland with the six northern counties being snatched away by a Union-Jack-sleeved hand. Another hand, with a tricolor sleeve, prevented the first hand from succeeding, and the slogan underlined the point, "Stad Maggie anois" ("Stop Maggie now").

After the hunger strike, as in the first wave of murals, the Beechmount area was remarkable for the quantity and overall quality of its murals. The international dimension of the armed struggle was captured, again in Beechmount Avenue, by two successive murals on the same wall. The first, in 1982, showed an IRA volunteer and a PLO soldier, both holding the same RPG rocket launcher. "PLO IRA, one struggle," added the caption. Four years later the international link celebrated was with black South Africa. Central to the mural was an ANC symbol and above it an armalite. "We aim to be free," a quotation from Bobby Sands, appeared on one side, and on the other a quotation from Bernard Maloise, recently executed in South Africa: "Tell the world freedom is at hand." The primacy of the armalite reveals the conviction that in both states, freedom only can occur through armed struggle.

Despite the growth in legitimacy of the republican movement after the hunger strike, it is clear from the murals that commitment to armed struggle has not weakened. When legalizing Sinn Féin in 1973, Secretary of State Merlyn Rees had hoped eventually to woo the party away from that commitment, to abandon the bullet for the ballot. But the movement was powerful and popular enough after the hunger strike to embrace both tactics. As Danny Morrison of the Ard

Fallswater Drive, 1982. Portrait of Padraic Pearse.

Chomharle of Sinn Féin stated at the 1981 Ard Fheis: "Will anyone here object if, with a ballot paper in one hand and the armalite in the other, we take power in Ireland?" (quoted in *An Phoblacht/Republican News*, 5 November 1981). The vast majority present did not object.

Thus the final message of the armed struggle murals was the Provisional IRA is "here to stay." It says as much in a 1982 mural in Twinbrook, and the message is emphasized by references to the phoenix and the year 1969. In an Islandbawn Street mural there are similar references—the lark and the year 1919, the first year of the IRA War of Independence. Consequently, a larger proportion of the post–hunger-strike murals have historical themes or allusions. The import of these is to emphasize that the struggle will continue until victory and that the IRA have the ultimate mandate for this armed struggle, their legitimate succession from republican activists of previous eras. For this reason some of the second wave of murals stressed this legitimacy using iconography, portraying the supreme heroes of the republican tradition. In 1982, on two walls within sight of each other in the Beechmount area, there were two murals depicting Patrick Pearse and James Connolly. The former mural included a quoatation from Pearse, "From the graves of patriot men and women spring living nations," and the latter a quotation from Connolly: "The great only appear great because we

Islandbawn Street, 1982. IRA 1919–1982; "We are here to stay."

Rossnareen Avenue, 1984. "An Slabhra gan Bhriseadh" ("The unbroken chain").

St. James Road, 1986. Cuchulain and memorial to dead local IRA volunteers; "I nDil Ċuimne" ("In loving memory").

are on our knees. Let us rise."

Pearse also figured, although anonymously, in a 1985 mural in Derry. It included in careful Celtic design the words of one of Pearse's poems, "Mise Éire," in which Ireland is compared with an old woman.

> I am Ireland,
> I am older than the old woman of Bearra,
> Great is my glory,
> I who gave birth to Cuchulain the brave,
> Great is my shame,
> My own family
> Have sold their mother.
> I am Ireland,
> I am lonelier than the old woman of Bearra.

The roots of the current struggle, for the mural artists as well as Pearse and Connolly, lie far back in history. Therefore, there is a notable predominance of Celtic designs and lettering in murals of this period. One of the first in this genre was a cluttered mural in Rosnareen Avenue, painted in 1984, showing a present-day IRA volunteer, a phoenix, and other symbols linked in "An slabhra gan bhriseadh—the unbroken chain." The accompanying message read

> We owe it to them,
> To those who have died,
> To those whose youth lies
> Battered against a prison wall,
> To our unborn children.

The chain thus links not just past and present, but also the future in an almost timeless struggle.

An ancient Celtic warrior appears in the "Mise Éire" mural. A similar warrior appears in two murals commemorating the deaths of more recent local heroes. The first, from 1985, is in Derry and contains a roll of honor of dead volunteers from the city. The second, from 1986, was painted in St. James Road and is accompanied by a plaque containing the names of dead volunteers from the area. The prominence of the Celtic warrior, as well as the traditional designs and symbols, points to the legitimate succession of these current heroes from those of the distant past. A small, simple mural in Andersonstown, dating from Easter 1986, makes a similar point, although less grandly. There is no list of names, only the symbol of death and the Easter Re-

Chamberlain Street, Derry, 1985. Firing party and phoenix.

Berwick Road, 1986. Blanketman on knees and (on boards) commemoration of 70th anniversary of Easter Rebellion.

Hawthorn Street, 1984. "Tiocfaidh Ár Lá" ("Our Day will come").

bellion, the lily, as well as the same slogan that appeared in the St. James mural: "I nDil Ċuiṁne" ("in loving memory"). This link with the dead volunteers of the past helps explain the

apparently anachronistic mural of 1985 in the Bogside, Derry, that returned to the hunger strike image of the final salute. But the hunger strike was by now part of that glorious history, a real event, but also one filled with almost mythical significance. In 1984 in Hawthorn Street, a reference to the hunger strike is also made; a quasi-mural carried merely the slogan of the H Blocks protesters: "Tiocfaidh Ár lá."

Finally, in Ardoyne the link with the hunger strike was stressed in another way. A 1981 mural depicting a naked blanketman was repainted in 1986, and above it on boards was painted a dying prisoner; two grieving women, one old and one young; and a reference that it was the 70th anniversary of the Easter Rebellion. Thus all the links were there, including the least obvious one that the design of the painting on boards was copied directly from a republican card issued in Easter 1972 at the height of internment.

MURALS: THE PROCESS

As has been emphasized throughout this chapter, the hunger strike of 1981 is the key to understanding the republican murals, not least because it inspired young people to turn to painting propaganda on the walls. One such person was Kes (involved in many of the murals in the Beechmount area, including the "Solidarity between women in armed struggle" mural mentioned earlier), then seventeen and just left school. Like most mural painters, he had had no art training, his sole experience being small-scale drawing at school. But with the hunger strike,

I felt something needed to be done and rather than go out and burn cars and throw stones, there was bound to be another action for the youth to put their views over. We founded a youth group and we started doing sponsored walks and sponsored runs and running discos to raise money to buy paint. We weren't dependent on anybody for any stuff, so we got the paint, and we asked people in their houses, "Any old paint?," for to donate it to us. And rather than mess the area up with dirty ould slogans, just "Smash H Block" and all, all over the place, we could do the same thing, put the same view across, only in an artistic way, and also clean up the area. We'd bring more support from the people seeing the youth aren't just out to burn and wreck the area." (transcript of taped interview, 4 November 1985)

Similarly, Digger, the artist who was behind all the murals in Ardoyne mentioned above as well as the Connolly mural in Beechmount and another in Divis Flats, was untrained. He had some graphic work experience, however, having drawn for various community and political magazines over the years. Although self-taught, he drew a kneeling blanketman that later became the central motif in a poster, an album cover, and a number of murals, including one of his own in Ardoyne.

There were a few artists with an art background. One was Joe Coyle in Derry, who had been involved in the 1970s in a few nonpolitical murals there, most notably a one hundred foot long by twenty foot high circus mural at the back of Rossville Flats. Five years later, Joe admitted that, although it had been an enjoyable experience at the time,

> it was a mistake for me to do it, in that it doesn't have any cultural identity in the local community. It's like a sort of plastic culture that has been implanted into people's heads. It's an international plastic Walt Disney-type culture that reflects in no way at all the culture of the local community. (transcript of taped interview with Julian Watson, 1982)

Joe's forte was to produce murals on eight-by-four-foot boards. This meant they were very mobile.

> They can be transported around, they can be used for stage backgrounds, they can be used for exhibition purposes and they can be put up just on a street corner if the need be for whatever purpose.

Derry, 1983. Election mural (on boards); "Vote Sinn Féin—Strike back at Thatcher."

Thus Joe's epic board mural likening the British task in Ireland to the self-defeating task of Sisyphus in the Greek myth appeared on a wall in Derry as well as some years later as the stage backdrop at a crucial Sinn Féin Ard Fheis in Dublin when the party voted to drop its abstentionist stance in relation to general elections in the South (see photograph in *An Phoblacht/Republican News*, 7 November 1986, p. 1). Later he also produced single board murals for Sinn Féin elections.

Despite his art training, ability, and innovativeness, Joe Coyle did not work alone; he worked alongside untrained young people. In that sense the Derry and Belfast experiences were similar; for the most part, young people with no art training discovered a talent and learned their skills on the job. As novices they were drawn to a collective form of operating out of sheer necessity. Kes describes how his mural team worked.

> There was three drawers and the rest were painters. So you got three people who could draw pretty good. They went out and drew it on the wall, using coloured chalk or white chalk, depending on what colour the background was gonna be, either black or white. We would chalk it out, then, to involve the whole group; the ones who couldn't draw, we would let them paint, so that we were bringing everybody in to do their fair share.

The lack of training had its advantages. A professional artist could well have been daunted by the scale of the paintings and the lack of tools and time to do the job. But the young amateurs showed remarkable ingenuity in getting around any obstacles. They rarely used conventional techniques. For example, they did not square the walls. One reason for this was that they did not have the luxury of spending weeks or months on a mural. Given the impending deaths of prisoners on hunger strike or an approaching election, the political message of the murals had to be broadcast urgently; in addition, potential harassment from passing police and army patrols made it preferable to finish as soon as possible. Instead of squaring the wall,

> it was better just to go ahead and chalk it out. What we done was we chalked it out, got down, looked at it. If it didn't look right, get up, rub a bit out, chalk it again, get down, just until it looked good and then we started painting it.

This can be seen clearly from the "Solidarity between Armed Women" mural on which Kes himself worked. The armalite chalked in above the women had not been drawn correctly, so it was erased and redrawn several times before emerging in its final form. No mechanical aids such as those used by mural artists elsewhere were used on this or any other mural; for example, projecting a slide on a wall to allow the artists to trace rather than draw. The murals were drawn free hand.

Finally, scaffolding was hard to obtain and

Falls Road, 1983. Solidarity between women in armed struggle mural; work in progress.

therefore rarely used. When available, it was usually of minimal use, providing only a relatively low platform from which to work. Instead, ladders were used, even for the largest murals. The "New Ireland" mural in Beechmount Avenue was completed by three teenagers with one short ladder and one longer one in only two days!

The young artists had a number of sources for inspiration, ranging from pure imagination (their own, as well as that of others) to copying existing images. As regards the latter, it has been pointed out already that sources as diverse as an Iranian poster and a photograph of an Official

Beechmount Avenue, 1983. "New Ireland" election mural; work in progress.

Hand-painted posters carried at head of hunger strike support march, 1981.

IRA volunteer taken in 1971 were used, as well as book and pamphlet covers, album sleeves, and political postcards. Similarly, the Moira Street mural on repression and resistance, mentioned earlier, was copied partly from a political postcard (also taken from a more widely known photograph) produced by Just Books in Belfast.

Interestingly, a political postcard of the latter mural appeared later, also produced by Just Books. This reveals another aspect of this visual culture, the cross-fertilization of ideas and images. Thus, the black coffins with white crosses that appeared in the early murals owe their origin to prehunger strike imagery produced by the Relatives Action Committees. In turn, these murals figured prominently in calendars produced by Republican Publications. In this way, one image could travel through a book or calendar, a poster, a postcard, a painting carried on a hunger strike march, as well as a mural.

Many of these images were highly original, including those whose sources were not related to the Irish struggle. Thus, silhouetted people appearing at the bottom of the 1986 "Revolution" mural in Beechmount (considered below) came from a film poster advertising the film *Reds*!

Among the most original images, in terms of their source if not their content, were those that emerged from the H Blocks. Drawn with colored pens on toilet paper or cigarette papers and smuggled out as "comms," these images once

"Comms" (communications) smuggled from Long Kesh prison; sketches of ideas for murals done on toilet paper. (Above), aspects of republican struggle, and (below) against the use of plastic bullets by the police and British army.

more revealed the close link between the murals and prison struggle. Few of them became fully fledged murals. One exception was a sketch that showed four people, among them a woman and a man holding a pick above his head. But the most prominent figure was a masked and armed IRA volunteer in the foreground. This sketch was later reproduced by Kes and a friend as a mural during an exhibition of Irish republican images at the Pentonville Gallery in London in 1983 (see Smith 1983). This is one of the few murals for which the record of a preliminary sketch seems to exist. This is mainly because preliminary sketches seem to have been rare, even for highly original murals. Moreover, once the mural itself existed, there seems to have been no urgency to keep the original sketch, if there was one.

A final aspect of the mural process is the effect of the murals on those viewing them. In the first wave of murals, the H Blocks/Armagh Committees were understandably very pleased with the work done by the youth groups. So also was Sinn Féin; as Kes puts it,

> they thought we were doing a great job, for we were drawing support for the movement and for the lads on the hunger strike.

Although not everyone in the areas where the murals were painted was a republican, it seems that the first murals at least were well received in nationalist areas. This had much to do with the extent of support that was finally mobilized for the hunger strikers. People who had never marched before or who had not done so since the days of civil rights were out on the streets alongside the traditional core of republican activists and supporters. So the circle was complete; the murals existed to mobilize support, and as the support grew, the murals had a receptive audience. Digger recalls that people in Ardoyne would "offer help and keep the cops off your back and would defend the mural." He became well known around the district, so that "loads of people who happened to live in gable houses came up and asked me: 'When are you doing the next one? Would you do one on my house?'"

Sometimes local affection for a mural could be on the most unexpected of grounds. Kes thought that the Sacred Heart mural in Beechmount on which he worked might have caused some of-

fence "with Our Lord in it and publicizing him with the fellows in the Blocks." But, on the contrary,

> that one brought a lot of goodwill from the people. The woman in the house, from what I heard, was going to ask the priest to bless it! That's true!

People in the local areas who may have disagreed with the contents of the murals, especially as they became more party political, kept their disagreement to themselves. The same cannot be said for the police and army. As Kes recalls, they would frequently mount the footpath in their jeeps and drive perilously close to the ladders on which the mural artists worked. More frequently, however, they inflicted the most damage at night by throwing "paint bombs"—plastic bags or bottles filled with paint—onto the murals. Sometimes this occurred long after a mural's completion. But some murals attracted a more rapid response. The PLO/IRA mural mentioned earlier was bombed with paint within hours of completion. Although repainted, the streams of white paint from the earlier paint bombing are clearly visible below the mural.

In this instance as in others, the artists returned after the attack to repair the mural. Kes claims that the police and army action did not demoralize his group.

> What I found with our youth movement was that the more they threw paint over them, the more determined we were going out to do them that wee bit better when we were cleaning them, and show the people that we weren't giving up easy, that we were here to stay.

On another occasion (quoted in Smith 1983), with tongue in cheek, he expressed gratitude to the paint bombers: "They've given me the power to practice on the walls. It's learning me how to paint!" Digger stressed another reason for the lack of demoralization.

> We felt that a mural shouldn't stay up very long. We should change it. Once you had got a certain supply of murals going, you should paint it out and do something different. (transcript of taped interview, 12 March, 1986)

So, as for police and army destruction,

> We expected it. The idea was to keep an ongoing

Cable Street, Derry, 1984. Mural portraying various aspects of republican struggle, plus quotation from Bobby Sands. (Courtesy: Elaine Thomas.)

Cable Street, Derry, 1984. Mural portraying various aspects of republican struggle, plus quotation from Bobby Sands; destroyed.

when it was only half completed. When repaired and finished, it lasted only one more day before it was damaged badly. It was left like that for a few months before being repaired again, and again was paint bombed. Finally, it was painted out in 1988 after being badly burnt by an August internment commemoration bonfire placed too close to it.

Leaving a destroyed mural in this condition was one way to publicize the pettiness of the police and army. On at least one occasion, in Derry's Bogside, the point was made more forcefully. The original mural showed hands of people carrying the various tools of their trade—a paint brush, a spanner, a book, and so on—in a style reminiscent of Latin American murals. Above them all was a hand bearing an armalite, depicting the primacy of the armed struggle. Accompanying the painting was a carefully painted quotation from Bobby Sands.

> Everyone, republican or otherwise, has his or her own particular part to play. No part is too great or too small. No one is too old or too young to do something.

Shortly after completion, this excellent mural was paint bombed. The vandals took the time to identify Bobby Sands as "slimmer of the year." The artists returned to the mural, not to repair it, but to add a plaque that stated simply:

> This mural was designed and painted by the creative talents of Derry republicans. It was vandalised by the destructive talents of the RUC and British army. July 1984.

Despite this harassment, no mural artist was injured by the police or army during the painting of a mural. In 1980 Michael McCartan, a sixteen-year-old youth in the Ormeau Road area of Belfast, was surprised by a police patrol one night as he painted the word "Provos" on a wall. He was shot dead.[18] A policeman, Constable McKeown, was charged with his murder, but found not guilty; part of his defense was that he believed McCartan was holding a gun. Some local people commemorated his acquittal by painting a large quasi-mural on a billboard near to where McCartan died. In addition to telling the story of McCartan's death and McKeown's acquittal, it sarcastically referred to the difference between a paint brush and an M60 heavy

mural thing going. It didn't really matter if we'd to go out and repair them.

But some murals were never repaired after a paint bomb attack. These attacks, combined with the ravages of weather, meant that by the mid-1980s few of the older murals were extant. On some occasions even recent murals were totally destroyed. Thus the 1986 "Revolution" mural in Beechmount Avenue was paint bombed

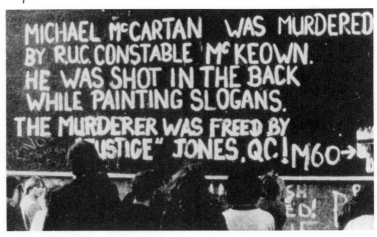

Ormeau Road, 1980. Protest message against freeing of policeman charged with murder of graffiti writer. (Courtesy: Siobhan Molloy.)

Cable Street, Derry, 1984. Mural portraying various aspects of republican struggle, plus quotation from Bobby Sands; plaque blaming police for destruction.

Oakman Street, 1981. Prisoners, and police shooting dead graffiti writer.

machine gun. When the murals emerged in 1981, a badly executed mural in Oakman Street referred to the event, linking Michael McCartan not merely to those dying in "Long Kesh prisoner of war camp" but also to those who forty years earlier had died in Auschwitz and Buchenwald. That only one mural artist died in such circumstances may have derived not only from the murder charge against Constable McKeown, but also from the quantity of muralists and the openness with which they painted. By 1981 there were too many mural artists to shoot, and because they worked in daylight by necessity, it was difficult for even the most short-sighted policeman to claim in his defense that he mistook a paint brush for a gun.

REPUBLICAN MURALS: A TRADITION IN THE MAKING?

In 1986, only five new republican murals were painted in Belfast, one or two in Derry, and one in Dublin. Although a massive decline from the heyday of five years earlier the appearance of any new murals at all is worth noting. Mural painting in nationalist areas, as mentioned earlier in this chapter, was not traditional. Before 1981, there were few nationalist murals. Furthermore, as a propagandistic intervention into a highly charged political situation, the murals of 1981 were not meant to be permanent.

Despite that, a brief explanation of the rapid decline of republican mural painting is necessary. At least one consideration was the cost of producing the murals. Logistically, as the fervor of the hunger strike subsided and the youth groups declined in numbers and importance, getting volunteers, money, and materials together to produce a mural became difficult. There also was an emotional cost involved; the systematic destruction of the murals by the police and army made it harder for most artists to muster the energy to begin again, despite what artists such as Kes and Digger conclude.

A second reason for the decline was the lack of specificity of focus for any new murals. The first wave of murals clearly related to the hunger strike and the second wave to the newfound popularity of Sinn Féin, particularly its electoral role. But as the hunger strike ended and Sinn Féin settled down to its acknowledged long and tedious road to success, the focus faded. There were still topics to paint about, particularly the continuing armed struggle, as well as many aspects of Sinn Féin's new social interest, for example, unemployment. But the murals on the former topic, especially in the Ballymurphy/Springhill area, became increasingly stark and clinical (one wit has referred to it as "armalite erotica"), and murals on the latter topic were regrettably and noticeably absent.

A third factor concerned those who produced the murals. The youth groups disintegrated as the hunger strike ended. Although some entered Sinn Féin, others did not. Some of those in Sinn Féin continued to paint murals occasionally, but there were many other tasks to be done—electoral work, advice giving, running the various departments of Sinn Féin, producing and distributing *An Phoblacht/Republican News;* these tasks took precedence.

Therefore, there was a contradiction involved in Sinn Féin becoming the major controller of republican murals. Murals frequently slipped down the agenda in importance, so when Sinn Féin attempted to encourage a mural revival, it had little success. Thus, in 1986 *An Phoblacht/Republican News* announced a mural competition; a £250 prize was offered to the artist of the best mural on a republican theme painted before the end of July (*An Phoblacht/Republican News,* 24 April 1986, 16). Despite reminding readers of the competition in subsequent issues and extending the deadline, the newspaper received less than a handful of entries.

At this low point of republican mural painting it might have seemed logical to conclude that the practice was dying out. The origins of republican mural painting were so specific relative to loyalist mural painting—propaganda around a hunger strike as opposed to the annual celebration of unionist triumph—that a short-lived history seemed inevitable. Certainly Digger almost implied this when he said that another mural explosion "would need some kind of campaign as strong as the hunger strike, but it's hard to see what that could be." But this misses the point that despite the problems in continuing the practice, the space has been created to allow those who feel they have a need and ability to propagandize from the walls to do so. Seventy years of loyalist mural painting has created a tradition; a republican practice lasting one tenth that time could hardly be called a tradition in the same sense, but the openness created in the past decade is a space into which people like Gerard Kelly can step easily.

Gerard is an exprisoner who had never painted before being jailed for a political offense. In prison, his painting mostly involved painstakingly copying the ornate interpretations of Celtic design and mythology of Jim Fitzpatrick (Fitzpatrick 1983). After Gerard's release, eight IRA volunteers were killed on 8 May 1987 in a carefully laid SAS (Special Air Services) ambush as they bombed an RUC station in Loughgall, County Armagh. Gerard was inspired to paint a memorial mural on a wall in Springhill Avenue close to his home. Unlike the muralists during the hunger strike, he took his time, squaring the wall and filling the whole space available. Over several weeks he painted a mural that was unique at the time in both its use of color and amount of detail. Six IRA volunteers stand to attention under a brightly colored Celtic cross. The rest of the wall is covered with the shields of the four provinces of Ireland, rolling hills, and rays of sun breaking through clouds. In Irish the mural notes the names of the eight dead volunteers and the time and manner of their deaths.

Encouraged by the success of this mural, Gerard returned to Jim Fitzpatrick's iconography for his next mural. In equally meticulous detail and color, he painted the warrior King Nuada, armed with sword and ready for action, surrounded by a dolmen, an ogham stone, and symbols of fire, water, cloudbursts, and green vegetation. As with the Loughgall painting, he covered the finished work (which took him more than three weeks to complete) with clear polyurethane varnish, thus ensuring that the murals could be repaired easily after the inevitable paint bombs. Unlike some previous mural artists, Gerard wanted his work to remain intact.

In the summer of 1987, Gerard also painted an election mural for Gerry Adams. Not only was this the first republican mural to depict an actual living person, it also was painted on the advertising hoarding at the corner of the Whiterock and Springfield Roads that had carried one of the first two republican murals of the 1981 period. That same summer, Gerard also painted three murals on Springhill Avenue: one based on a Cormac cartoon in *An Phoblacht/Republican News,* another based on the cover of Cormac's "col-

Springhill Avenue, 1987. Cartoon mural.

lected works" (Information on Ireland 1982), and a third based on the cover of Bob Marley's "Uprising" album, the first and only time to date that both Marley and the Rasta colors appeared in a Belfast mural.

Gerard was equally busy in 1988. Working quickly this time, he produced a mural memorial to the three IRA volunteers Mairead Farrell, Danny McCann, and Sean Savage, killed by the SAS in Gibraltar on 6 March 1987. The design was copied from an album cover (which was copied from the cover of a pamphlet [Macardle n.d.]) depicting a roadside monument in Ballyseedy, near Tralee, County Kerry. This monument was erected in 1959 in commemoration of a horrific incident during the Civil War when Irish Free State soldiers tied nine captured republican guerrillas to a bomb and exploded it, killing all but one. Like the monument, Gerard's mural shows a mother holding an infant, both of whom look down on a dead or dying man; another man, his face set in determination, strides off intent on revenge. This mural, completed during three days of incessant heavy rain, shows

Springfield Road, 1987. Election mural for Gerry Adams, M.P.

signs of haste, including the fact that the quotation from Mairead Farrell—"I have always believed we had a legitimate right to take up arms"—was painted carefully indoors on strips of wood and nailed to the wall minutes before her funeral began.

The next month, Gerard painted a mural on the Easter Rising that depicts some of the care, style, and love of color evident in his first two murals. Surrounded by the busts of the seven signatories of the Declaration of Independence in 1916 stands the dying Cuchulain, tied to a post, as mythology has it, so he could die upright. Alongside are the words of Padraic Pearse's poem "Mise Éire." The whole frame is filled with the colors of sea, mountains, grass, and a sunburst. Shortly afterward, Gerard's liking for Cormac's work emerged again. Cormac had drawn an epic cartoon parodying a government campaign to encourage people to use the confidential telephone to the police. The cartoon reversed the message by urging people to telephone Sinn Féin advice centers when harassed by the police or army. Gerard copied this cartoon on a gable wall in Ballymurphy, the wall that had the first republican mural in 1981.

On the New Lodge Road, Gerard also painted a huge portrait of local man Joe Doherty, held in the United States under threat of extradition. Like his earlier painting of Adams, this mural broke with tradition by depicting a living person, as did his next mural, painted on the eve of Nelson Mandela's 70th birthday in the summer of 1988. The style was simple and not immediately recognizable as Gerard's, but the quality of the artwork and the careful balance of color marks it as one of his most effective paintings.

This mural received much praise when viewed by Irish artist Robert Ballagh, who was in Belfast in August 1988 to judge a mural competition as part of the first West Belfast community festival. One of Gerard's murals, that of King Nuada at Springhill Avenue, won.

Gerard's entries were not the only ones in the competition, however. Although the most prolific, competent, and famous of republican mural artists, he is not alone. Others have been responsible for at least a dozen murals in Belfast in 1988. The most favorite theme is the armed struggle, thus they differ from Gerard's murals

Whiterock Road, 1988. Cartoon mural.

New Lodge Road, 1988. Joe Doherty, held in U.S. prison on basis of extradition warrant from Britain.

Falls Road, 1988. Nelson Mandela mural; Irish artist Robert Ballagh pictured along with two of the young artists in the foreground.

with its wide range of themes. More noticeable is the predominance of images of masked volunteers. Although the anonymous Green Beret-type volunteer of 1981 (mentioned earlier) was resurrected on a wall in South Link in 1988 and a nearby mural depicts three unmasked volunteers on patrol, most of these murals are more sinister. In Upper Meadow Street, beside a quotation from Bobby Sands, an armed volunteer wearing a black balaclava poses in front of a map of Ireland. A balaclava also features centrally in a Falls Road mural at the same time. Better executed, but still featuring a balaclava and masks, is a Twinbrook mural showing two armed volunteers in action and ten volunteers, including two women, standing to attention. One of the few armed struggle murals of this period to break from the oppressive obsession with masks is the mural memorial in Turf Lodge to local man Kevin McCracken, killed in action in March 1988. Accompanying a portrait of McCracken are the words of two verses of a popular political song written by Jack Warshaw, "No Time for Love," one of which was

Falls Road, 1988. Armed IRA man and shields of four provinces of Ireland; "Freedom's Sons."

> Come all you people who give to your comrades
>   the will to fight on,
> They say you can get used to this war, that
>   doesn't meant that this war isn't on.
> The fish need the sea to survive just like your
>   comrades need you
> And the death squad can only get through to
>   them if first they can get through to you.

It is tempting to attribute this obsession with masks to a return to traditional republican concerns and away from the newfound community politics of posthunger strike Sinn Féin. A more important explanation is probably the lack of ability of the artists. It is clear from most of the murals of the period other than Gerard Kelly's that the ability is lackluster. Painting volunteers with masks is easier than painting facial features. In this regard, it is important to note that the highly competent Kevin McCracken mural just mentioned was painted by someone with art college training.

Beyond the immediate reference to the armed struggle, two murals in Belfast in 1988 referred to the plight of republican prisoners. By this time, 25 percent of the North's prisoners were serving life sentences; many of these had spent

Gardenmore Road, 1988. IRA volunteer with RPG rocket launcher, and other volunteers standing to attention.

Norglen Gardens, 1988. Memorial to IRA man Kevin McCracken, plus chorus of "No Time for Love."

Laburnham Way, 1988. Mural in support of campaign for release of life sentence prisoners.

Lenadoon Walk, 1988. Silhouette of defiant prisoner and Long Kesh prison.

15 or more years in prison with no clear assurance through current review procedures as to when they might be released (Rolston and Tomlinson 1988). A campaign on behalf of these lifers was built around six proposals, and these featured prominently in a mural in Laburnum Way. Also featured was the lark in barbed wire, the symbol made famous in the early murals during the hunger strike of Bobby Sands.[19] The

CONCLUSION

There is, to use the title of Curtis's (1984) book,

Cable Street, Derry, 1987. "Bua" (Victory).

other mural referring to prisoners was in Lenadoon Avenue and showed a prisoner in silhouette giving a clenched fist salute as he towered above Long Kesh prison.

In Derry, too, the tradition was kept alive with new murals now and again. Perhaps the most unusual is one painted at Cable Street in 1987. Copied from the painting by Joan Miro for the cover of a 1937 French anti-fascist pamphlet *Aidez l'Espagne*, it is the least conventional of all republican murals. It shows a stylized figure giving a clenched fist salute. The Derry artists took the liberty of adding one word in Irish—"bua" ("victory"). Another mural with international connections appeared on the same wall the following year. Che Guevara and Lenin stood alongside Bobby Sands and IRA volunteers.

These republican murals are tied to an ongoing armed struggle that has relatively stable support in nationalist working class communities. As such the murals are not ritualistic in the way that loyalist murals traditionally were, tied solely to the annual celebration of the key event in loyalist political culture, the Twelfth. Instead, republican mural artists are inspired by current events or connections they can make with struggles elsewhere to paint propaganda on walls in their communities.

a "propaganda war" in progress in Northern Ireland. Like the wider military conflict of which it is part, this war pitches antagonists against each other using the weapons they have at hand, including the media, which is the specific object of Curtis's study. Her conclusion is that, despite an initial sympathy for Northern nationalists, the British media settled down quickly within a few years of the emergence of the "troubles" into a consensual view of the North that has been pro-British, prounion (even if not noticeably pro-unionist), and antirepublican.

But a war requires more than one protagonist. The dominant British consensus about the North of Ireland thus has been challenged by many nationalists, republicans, socialists, civil libertarians, and others. Republicans in particular have had clear definitions of the war that have run counter to those of the British state. Unlike the state, however, they have not had the same access to large-scale, high-tech information systems to disseminate their definitions.

The propaganda war has raged over interpretations of events, representations of history, and even the words used—"terrorist" versus "freedom fighter," for example. The war has also had its visual component. We have already noted in this chapter how the BBC had only one photograph of Bobby Sands which, despite their dislike of it for representing him as a likeable human being, they broadcast reluctantly. Thus they provided an image for mass consumption that was used widely by republican mural painters committed to an entirely different assessment of Sands and his actions.

The Northern Ireland Office, learning the lesson of photographic images, made a more definitive intervention later in the hunger strike. "Fact Sheets" were produced and circulated widely to local and particularly to foreign media. Each fact sheet concerned an individual hunger striker. Purporting to be an objective statement, it reproduced excerpts from newspapers that covered the "terrorist" incident(s) for which the person had been convicted as well as the trial. In each case there was an accompanying photograph, and these photographs were far from flattering. They were clearly from police files and had obviously been taken at the time of the person's arrest and detention after long hours of interrogation (under the Prevention of Terrorism Act and the Emergency Provisions Act, suspects can be held and interrogated for seven days,

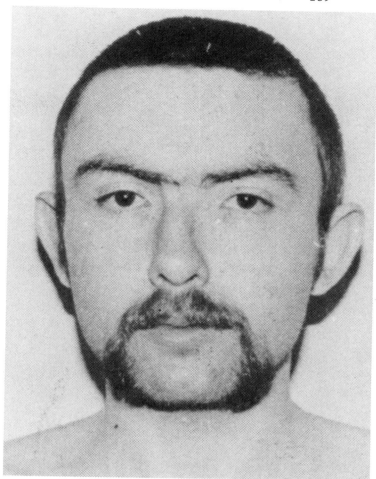

Fact File, 1981. Northern Ireland government photograph of hunger striker; detail of press release.

without legal counsel, before being released or charged). The combination of fatigue and unwillingness to be photographed shows on prisoners' faces. These are not objective images, but ones that visually convey directly and immediately the dominant definitions of the struggle; these men are clearly "ruthless terrorists." These are the images the Northern Ireland Office propaganda machine wanted distributed world wide. The warmer, folksier, more human representations of these men by the republican movement were confined to posters, postcards, pamphlet covers, and murals. None were as amenable to global consumption as the Northern Ireland Office images.

Although this propaganda war is unbalanced, the British state has been known to interfere

"Freedom '74"; republican poster in support of armed struggle and release of internees from Long Kesh.

directly with the images produced by republicans. For example, in 1974 republicans produced a poster showing an armed IRA volunteer and internees being released from Long Kesh. It also contained the caption "Freedom '74." In a classic Kitsonian move (Kitson 1971), a counter-propaganda unit of the British army reprinted this poster and pasted it on walls throughout West Belfast; after the caption they had added the message, "but not from the barrel of a gun."

In the same vein, we have already considered the extent to which murals have been destroyed by police and army paint bombs. On at least two

occasions, however, British army personnel have been more ambitious in their use of paint; they have painted murals themselves. In 1972, a crudely painted mural was done in Raglan Street as part of the Gloucester Regiment's farewell to the residents at the end of their four-month tour of duty. On the same night they hoisted a Union Jack flag over a local cinema, sounded the last post, fired shots in the air, and raided a number of homes, they also painted a Union Jack surrounded by a roll call of battle fields—Aden,

"Freedom '74"; as previous republican poster, but after changes added by British army counter-propaganda unit.

South Link, 1988. IRA volunteers in action; "Beidh ár Lá Linn" ("Our day will come").

Falls Road, 1988. Our Lady, Star of the Sea.

Cyprus, India, Kenya, Palestine, Malaya and Ireland (see *Irish News,* 12 April 1972). More ambitious was the mural painted inside an army base overlooking Derry's Bogside. It shows the silhouettes of four British soldiers armed and preparing for action, and it is clearly copied from a republican mural on the wall of the Bogside Inn below, itself copied from a mural that had been in Beechmount Avenue, Belfast, the only difference being that in the latter two murals the figures were of IRA volunteers (see the cover of *Soldier,* 13 June 1988). The British army mural bore the slogan "Oglaigh na h-Howards," which the editor of *Soldier,* showing his ignorance of both the Irish language and republican slogans, translated as "Our day will come—Green Howards" (the Green Howards being the British army regiment to whom the painting of the mural was attributed).[20] "Oglaigh" is the Irish word for "volunteers," and "Oglaigh na hÉireann" is the Irish name for the IRA. The Irish for "our day will come" is "tiocfaidh ár lá."

Recently, another apparently unlikely institution has begun to play a part in this visual propaganda war—the Catholic church. On 25 April 1988, some youths began a mural in South Link, Andersonstown. It depicted eight armed IRA volunteers carrying or using various weapons, including a drogue bomb, a highly effective

homemade hand grenade packed with the high explosive Semtex. That night the local parish priest, aided by a nun, obliterated the military figures by painting over them with black paint (*Andersonstown News,* 30 April 1988). The young artists later repainted their mural, but one less able mural nearby, which portrayed a masked man with a drogue bomb and which had also been clerically vandalized, was not repainted.

Elsewhere in Belfast, at least four murals on religious themes were painted in 1988 with Catholic church sponsorship. Two were in Upper Meadow Street: one depicted Our Lady of Medjugorje (a popular place of pilgrimage in Yugoslavia), and the other the Lamb of God, bathed in light from heaven, waiting to be sacrificed on an altar. In Clonard Street, in the car park of a monastery, the appearance of Our Lady to three children at Fatima, Portugal, in 1917 was depicted. At the bottom of the Falls Road, on the side of a hostel for the homeless, was the largest of these murals, depicting Our Lady, Star of the Sea.

Art is clearly a much used weapon in the propaganda war in Northern Ireland, and its use shows no sign of waning as the war enters its third decade. While that is so, it seems there will continue to be republicans willing to take up that weapon.

4

Political Murals:
International Perspectives

MURALS AND THE STRUGGLE FOR
NATIONAL INDEPENDENCE

Mention of political murals immediately brings to mind Mexico in the 1920s. During that period established painters—most prominent among them being David Alfaro Siqueiros, Diego Rivera, and Jose Clemente Orozco—were sponsored by the revolutionary government of Alvaro Obregon to paint monumental murals on the walls of many prominent buildings. Despite major differences in style and approach—Rivera's deceptive simplicity, Siqueiros's gigantic figurative style, and Orozco's almost mystical introspection—each sought in his own way to produce art portraying the revolutionary struggle of the Mexican people for national independence.

As the Mexican muralists lent their skills to the service of the revolution in the 1920s, across the Atlantic the state of Northern Ireland was born out of the partition that followed an unsuccessful struggle for national independence. During that decade, political mural painting was common in the new state as it had been for more than a decade previously in the area. The names of the Mexican muralists are well known to this day, but those of the past mural painters of Northern Ireland are not, even within the loyalist communities in which they painted, except

to those with an interest in the subject.

It is tempting to explain the fame of one set of muralists and the oblivion of the other merely in terms of skill. The Mexican muralists were not only established artists in their own right, but when they turned to mural painting they continued to produce work regarded as artistically superior. The loyalist murals of Northern Ireland were painted mostly by working class men, who at most had the skills of coach painters or house decorators. Then as now few established artists in Ireland were prepared to commit themselves so politically in their art.

In relation to Northern Ireland's traditional murals, the question is, to what would the artists have committed themselves? In Mexico, artists threw their lot in with the struggle for national independence and thus became both reflectors of and contributors to the revolutionary change in Mexican society. In doing so, they built on a cultural identity that had been articulated in the decades before—rejecting the old forms imposed by dependency and forging new images of themselves and their nation, especially through a rediscovery and reinterpretation of Indian culture. A remarkably similar phenomenon had occurred in Ireland in the same period

112

with the rediscovery and reinterpretation of Celtic culture. As in the Mexican case, established artists, particularly playwrights and poets rather than visual artists, had been an integral part of the forging of a new national identity and consciousness. But the mural painters of Northern Ireland were not part of this national movement. As unionists they were part of the community that saw its economic and political future in terms of the link with Britain. Partition occurred to preserve that link. The unionists found few intellectuals to side with their cause. It was a less grand cause, literally a reactionary one, geared toward preserving the union against all odds. As such, it attracted the empathy and support of British army officers and out-of-office Conservative Party politicians but of few Irish intellectuals.

This is how the Mexican and Northern Ireland murals differ most. It is not just that the former are "art" and the latter, even at their best, could never have been awarded such an accolade. Rather, it is that the Mexicans were on the side of a successful nationalist revolution. The Irish muralists sided with those in whose interests the full national revolution was thwarted. The analogy would be to imagine that somehow Siqueiros, Rivera, and Orozco lent their skills to praise the achievements of the dictator Porfirio Diaz, rather than the popular movement that overthrew him. What would their themes have been then? How revolutionary in content and style would their art have been? The questions are unanswerable because the analogy is ludicrous. The Mexican muralists drew their strength, energy, and inspiration from the national struggle of which they were an integral part. The muralists of Northern Ireland were part of a group that saw the Irish national revolution as the very antithesis of their culture and identity.

Sixty years after the formation of the state, the minority community in Northern Ireland undertook mural painting with a passion and energy that surprised everyone. The trigger for this explosion of mural painting was the republican hunger strike during which ten prisoners starved to death. Those who painted republican murals, mostly young men, were to first appearances similar to their working class counterparts who traditionally had been painting loyalist murals throughout this century. But the content and style of their murals reveal important differences. With a few exceptions in recent years, loyalist murals have been splendidly predictable, depicting either crossed flags or other inanimate symbols, or the defeat by Protestant King William III of Catholic King James IV at the Battle of the Boyne in 1690. Republican murals have had a wider range of themes—the hunger strike, elections, issues of repression—and a flexibility in their approach that allows for less predictable images. Thus like the annual 12 July celebration of William's victory at the Boyne, the loyalist murals, painted as an essential part of those celebrations, have been ritualistic. Tied less to a real or mythical event, republican murals have been more imaginative. Ultimately, such imagination derives from the republican muralists' incorporation in the struggle waged by the republican movement as a whole. Considering their identity as part of an age-old struggle for national independence, republicans have no problem linking Ireland's celtic past (history, language, mythology) with national liberation struggles elsewhere (Nicaragua, Palestine, South Africa). Republican muralists therefore have a wide repertoire to chose from in presenting that identity in visual form.

In this sense only, republican muralists appear to be close to the Mexican muralists of an earlier generation. Both have been active participants in a liberation struggle and have used their artistic skills to further the cause. But there are enough differences between them to make this comparison faulty as well. The republican painters of Northern Ireland are not and will never be established artists, because they see themselves as revolutionaries using art as a weapon, not artists "doing their bit" for the revolution. Untrained and sometimes remarkably nonreflective about their work, they have learned to use this weapon on the job, in the heat of battle as it were.

ART AND REVOLUTION

The Mexican muralists, despite the obstacles in their paths from time to time, were paid cultural workers of a revolutionary order that was well on the way to survival. It was ten years after Diaz's demise before the Minister of Education, Jose Vasconcelos, began to sponsor murals. Although murals had been painted before then, they were not the major phenomenon that they then became. Mexico in the throes of revolutionary change was not committed to largescale sponsorship of mural art.

Kavolis (1965, cited in Rodriguez 1974, p. 139) argues that "artistic creativity is maximized not during but immediately after periods of most intensive political action." The Mexican case bears this out, as does the other revolution to which at least two of the three Mexican muralists looked for political inspiration, the Soviet Union. After the October Revolution, many artists produced art for the new Russia with an incredible enthusiasm. Gray (1962, p. 220) notes that although the fight for the survival of the revolution against internal and external forces had to continue for some years, and the artists like most other citizens were actually hungry, they hardly seemed aware of the grimness of the present. "Euphoria" is the word Gray (1962, p. 226) uses to describe projects such as Tatlin's proposed monument to the Third International; it was to be twice as high as the Empire State building, and yet the whole structure was to revolve! The grandeur, scale, and recklessness of the project would come to represent the Soviet transformation itself. This euphoria did not result from blindness regarding the hardship of the present, but rather from a faith in the revolution's ability to overcome this hardship as it would overcome all other obstacles to the creation of the new society.

The enthusiasm of visual artists specifically is evident in the magnificent Soviet film posters produced at the time. Constantine and Fern's (1974, p. 7) conclusion is that in art, as in politics, the Soviet revolution seemed to jump stages; "from having few posters, and not very interesting ones, the Soviet production became one of the most fascinating in the world"—not least in terms of the innovative styles invented by the graphic artists.

A similar phenomenon is apparent in other socialist revolutions. An artistic transformation occurred in Portugal, Nicaragua, and Grenada,[1] and in at least the first two cases, murals were the most visible evidence of that explosion. The postrevolution transformation of art in these societies was in terms of its de-bourgeoisification, its popular production and its quantity. Writing of prerevolutionary Portugal under Salazar, for example, Velez (1964) spells out the problems facing the Communist Party in producing oppositionalist propaganda. In a situation in which any signs of public dissent were suppressed quickly, ingenious ways of communication were invented. For example, leaflets were stuffed into the exhausts of stationary cars from which they were blown out as the cars drove away. Given the totalitarian nature of the state, there was no possiblity of painting murals. Yet, not much more than a decade later, everything had changed. Countless walls in Portugal were painted with murals not only by the Communist Party (see Nissen 1976) but be every progressive, communist, and anarchist party or group (see *As Parades Na Revolucao*, 1978; Grasskamp and Kottek 1982).

In Nicaragua, the emergence from a long period of dictatorship under the Somoza dynasty led to a similar mural explosion. Here, as La Duke (1984a, p. 46) notes, established easel painters such as Alejandro Canales turned to mural painting after the Sandinista victory; he had never painted a mural before, but "necessity forces one to learn." Ordinary Nicaraguans[2] were learning the skills too, as evidenced by the profusion of murals in every town and village. Another sign of the popularity of mural painting was the production of a Sandinista instruction manual on the techniques and political importance of mural painting (Departamento de Propaganda y Educacion del FSLN 1981).

On a lesser scale, Grenada's revolution also produced an outburst of artistic activity. La Duke (1984b) concludes that the popularity of Maurice Bishop and his People's Revolutionary Government were at the root of this outburst. Previously art had been a minor, elitist, and Europeanized activity, the only exception being the production of "folk art" for tourists. But now ordinary people were producing art, realizing their creative potential and showing in this and in other ways their identification with the goals and successes of the government.

The Grenadian revolution did not outlast the U.S. invasion of October 1983. The Nicaraguan revolution has barely survived, given the weight of an economic embargo imposed by the United States and a U.S.-sponsored dirty war undertaken by the contras. For the Nicaraguans, as for many political propagandists, another Latin American revolution brought down through U.S. intervention has been held up as an example of the odds facing socialist revolutionaries. Chile's democratically elected Marxist government under Salvador Allende was overthrown in September 1973 after only three years of existence. With the coup, one of many popular forms of struggle and consciousness-raising smashed was the recent but lively tradition of mural painting. Allende's election led to an upsurge in the production of images supporting the Popular Unity government, including posters, comic books, and murals. By 1973, Kunzle (1978, p. 363) estimates there were 150 mural brigades in Chile. These Ramona Parra Brigades of the Communist Party (named after a young militant killed in 1949) were organized as collectives with a highly specialized division of labor. A *trazador* traced the outlines of the symbols, a *rellenador* filled in the colors of the symbols, a *fondeador* painted the background, a *filetador* added the outlines and contours, and a *retocador* did any touching up required. Up to twelve people were involved in a mural team. The result was an efficient collective machine that could produce a large mural at amazing speed. As in Mexico, Nicaragua, and Portugal, these muralists worked on behalf of the newly successful socialist revolution. Their vitality and enthusiasm thus would confirm Kavolis's conclusion, already quoted, that "artistic creativity is maximized . . . immediately after periods of most intensive political action." But the style, speed, and relative lack of sophistication of the murals raises the question of why legitimate cultural workers, supporting a popular revolution, should have acted this way. The answer, of course, is that the manner of producing murals derived from an earlier period, before the Popular Unity government had come to power. The

speed and collective labor were necessary survival techniques in a situation in which painting oppositionalist propaganda on the walls could lead to harassment if not death. The painters acted like "guerrilla muralists" (Kunzle 1978, p. 363) after Allende's success, because that is how they had been required to act beforehand.

Thus Chilean mural painting went through three phases. In the turmoil of the Christian Democrat government before Allende's victory, murals were produced in a semi-clandestine manner, mainly under the auspices of the Communist Party. After Allende's victory, there was a brief flowering of open propaganda, no longer oppositionalist, but now in support of the revolutionary state. As Vicuna (1974) recounts, ordinary people turned to cultural propaganda work, and established artists such as herself had their eyes opened to produce art in the service of the revolution. But the cultural explosion was as short-lived as the Popular Unity government itself. After Allende's overthrow, mass repression was imposed. Many cultural workers, including muralists, fled the country and continued to paint their anti-Junta murals in exile. Oppositionalist propaganda, however, continued under the Junta. As Dorfmann (1983) notes, jokes have become a major vehicle of resistance, with up to three years imprisonment possible for anti-government humor. Despite such repression, alternative cultural activities go on, even in the prisons under the eyes of the regime. Dorfmann (1983, p. 203) concludes

> . . . one must not forget—and the Junta does not forget—that the Chilean resistance is a resistance of masses. Herein lies its force . . . It is precisely the popular, massive character of these manifestations which limits the possibilities of repressing or even of keeping watch on them.

Chile's murals, therefore, are in a different category from those of Mexico, Nicaragua, and Portugal. For all but a three-year period, they have not been state-approved cultural work, but vibrant oppositionalist propaganda, parallel with the republican murals of the 1980s in Northern Ireland. The collective labor, the relative lack of sophistication in content and technique, the lack of expensive paints and tools—all of these characteristics of Chilean murals would be familiar to republican mural painters. Similarly, they would identify with Dorfmann's conclusion that, as part of a wider mass movement, they ultimately cannot be prevented from producing oppositionalist art. There are too many of them to kill.

Lacking the legitimacy conferred by an established revolution, socialist or nationalist, republican muralists in Northern Ireland are similar to those in Chile in another sense. Neither has had to face the dilemma of how individual artist and revolutionary state can achieve a modus vivendi in the long run. From the newly established revolutionary state's point of view, there often is a simplistic conclusion drawn that art must equal uncritical propaganda, otherwise it is the work of bourgeois individualists and counter-revolutionaries. The dilemma can be solved in a simple way. Artists can be required to produce propaganda that at its worst is ponderous, as in the heavy didactic billboards of Grenada mentioned by La Duke (1984b), or at best heroic and uncritical.

This solution was prefigured in the creation of the notion of "socialist realism" under Stalin in the USSR. The tension between artists wanting independence and the state requiring graphic functionaries was evident as early as 1921. Artists supporting independence and yet committed to the revolution were organized in Proletcult—the Organisation for Proletarian Culture. They opposed moves by the People's Commisariat for Education to centralize all cultural production under state control. As Gray (1962, p. 245) notes, the fight was only fully lost in 1932 when socialist realism became the one official style and all artistic organizations were gathered under one central body, the Union of Artists. The effect on the production of innovative film posters as well as other cultural products was apparent. Even the most prolific artists, such as the Sternberg Brothers, turned from experimentation to conventional representation. As Constantine and Fern (1974, p. 15) conclude, "The mandate to create a revolutionary art was withdrawn," and the antagonism between artist and state was solved to the benefit of the state.

Art was relegated to a similar subsidiary role in the China of the Cultural Revolution, as Fraser (1977, p. 3) concludes:

> Mass-produced poster art in China is a controlled medium, and though there is an increasing

number of works appearing which do have an obvious or total political message, the initiation, commissioning, production and dissemination of poster art is the acknowledged political responsibility of the government . . .

Stermer (1970) adds that at least the Chinese did not imitate the Russians by depriving the mass of the people of any role in the production of this art.

Revolutionary art in Mexico also waned. As revolutionary zeal faded, the one-party state no longer wanted reminders of their abandonment of ideals. Orozco became more and more cynical; Rivera went back to the Communist Party from which he had been expelled; Siquieros ended up in prison between 1960 and 1964. Grieb (1984) notes that by the 1970s, under the presidency of Luis Echeverria Alvarez, Mexico City's walls sported nothing grander than slogans painted to order. Officially commissioned, these paintings, mainly in working-class areas, offered advice on health, education, and so on, or more generally pro-government and broadly nationalist aphorisms. These equivalents of party political posters or government health advertisements were far from the grandeur of the earlier murals.

Writing in 1950 against socialist realism as a solution to the tension between art and revolution, Trotsky (1975, p. 29) argued

> A revolutionary party is neither able or willing to take upon itself the task of "leading" and even less of commanding art, either before or after the conquest of power . . . Art, like science, not only does not seek orders, but by its very essence cannot tolerate them.

Thus Trotsky was taking a clear stand on the "art versus the state" conflict, unlike Stalin, siding with the former rather than the latter. His position influenced Diego Rivera in Mexico, to the point that Rivera, Trotsky, and Andre Breton produced a Manifesto in Support of Free, Revolutionary Art in 1938.

It is unlikely that Trotsky's ideas influenced the revolutionaries of Nicaragua or Cuba. But it is clear that they concluded, as he did, that the revolutionary state must trust those artists who support the revolution to find their own ways to express and develop that support. In Nicaragua, as Waller (1987, p. 8) puts it, "the Stalinist notion of the artist being subservient to a political line is refreshingly absent." At the same time, as Cope (1987, pp. 12–13) adds, there was a move away from elitism, and a commitment to the principle that "in cultural matters the people are the experts" marks a change in Sandinista policy. Initially the Sandinistas

> concentrated on providing access to a bank of artists whose skills could be called upon by mass organisations. Now the new system encourages local popular cultural expression in whatever form seems most appropriate in each area.

The path of allowing artists the freedom to experiment within the overall revolutionary movement has been followed consistently by the Cuban authorities, at least in relation to posters, as Sontag (1970, p. xv) argues. There are two opposing views on the role of art in revolution.

In one, art expresses and explores an individual sensibility. In the other, art serves a social-political or ethical aim. To the credit of the Cuban revolution, the contradiction between these two views has **not** been resolved.

The result was that poster artists took the opportunity to produce work that was aesthetically as well as politically sound.

In this sense, Cuban posters came close to Benjamin's (1982, p. 214) ideal that a work of art with correct politics must necessarily be of good artistic quality. Such an ideal rarely has been achieved. Even in Cuba other artists, particularly poets, have not had as comfortable a relationship with the state as have the poster artists. That apart, Sontag praises the uniqueness of the Cuban solution to the tension between art and revolution, namely, "**not** to come to any particular solution, not to put great pressure on the artist."

SPONSORSHIP AND INDEPENDENCE

As the example of the USSR shows, the revolutionary state is in a good position to put pressure on the dissenting artist if it judges that art must be the slave of politics. Art requires an outlet and usually also sponsorship. When the state can control access to both of these resources, the artist must choose between obeying or ceasing to produce art.

Sponsorship is of crucial importance in other than revolutionary societies, too. A key example is that of the United States in the 1930s. In 1933, the Treasury Department set aside money for a Public Works of Art Project (PWAP) whereby artists were hired to produce art for federal buildings. The Project lasted less than a year, but more than 15,000 pieces of art were produced, including approximately 400 completed murals. The success of PWAP led to the creation of the Fine Arts Section of the Treasury in 1938 in which sponsorship of public art continued. Parallel to these activities was the Federal Art Project, a section of the Works Progress Administration, and therefore designed more clearly as relief work for destitute artists during the depression. It had fourteen times as much money as the Fine Arts Section and aided ten times as many artists. In 1943, all such funding

of public art ended, because of the decline of Roosevelt's New Deal philosophy and the preparations for war. Such federal sponsorship was not resurrected until 1963.

The Fine Arts Section was highly centralized and bureaucratic; its director, Edward Bruce, was adamant that he wanted, in the words of McKinzie (1972, p. 57), "representational competence, the ability to render detail literally," and the skills of the "academic artist applied to wholesome American themes." For the most part Bruce got precisely this, a New Deal Realism to match the socialist equivalent developing elsewhere at the same time. In relation to murals specifically, public buildings (particularly post offices) throughout the United States abounded in Norman Rockwell-like images of happy farmers, well-fed laborers, and heroic pioneers. Despite Bruce's tight control—no nudes, no nightmares for children, no modernism, and no communist propaganda—some murals caused controversy. Most obvious was that around Coit Tower in San Francisco (see McKinzie 1972, pp. 23–27). In one panel a miner read the *Western Worker*, a Communist Party weekly. Books by Marx could be detected on library shelves. Another panel contained a hammer and sickle and the slogan "Workers of the world unite." Yet another showed unpleasant details of street life, including a hold-up and a riot. The public outcry over such murals leads McKinzie (1972, p. 27) to conclude that, although murals "comprised less than 3% of the items produced . . . they commanded disproportionate attention."

The same conclusion may be reached in relation to the Federal Art Project murals. This Project was much less bureaucratic than that of the Fine Arts Section, and perhaps for that reason it had a more turbulent history (see McKinzie 1972, 165–66). Some of the 2,566 murals produced stirred up controversy. The administrator of one mural project in New York City was dismissed for approving a mural that displayed a pair of calipers and a micrometer, supposedly arranged to suggest the Soviet emblem. Another mural, painted on panels, was officially burned because one figure looked suspiciously like Lenin. A mural at Newark Airport was said to have shadows painted that formed the numbers "441," the numbers of New York's Communist Party local branch. Murals at Harlem Hospital painted by black artists and depicting aspects of black history and culture led to official censorship and opposition (see Berman 1977).

It was thirty years before federal support for public art was reinstituted. In 1963 the Treasury agreed that no more than half a percent of the overall cost of construction of a federal building could be devoted to artistic embellishment. Such funding ceased in 1966 after a dispute over a mural at Kennedy Airport, but it was reinstated in 1972; between then and 1979 federal funding supported 91 completed art works, including eight murals. Thalacker's (1980) conclusion that current sponsorship of art in public places had begun to rival that during the 1930s is exaggerated. At the same time, it is clear that the 1970s project had at least one similarity with the 1930s; namely, murals comprised a small proportion of the finished works but often aroused controversy. For example, in Texas mural artist Roberto Rios planned two murals for the interior of the Border Patrol headquarters. One was to show Mexicans working in the United States and others pointing at them from across the Rio Grande. The proposal was rejected because it seemed to encourage illegal immigration. The

other mural proposal was accepted without criticism and was painted eventually: it praised the work of the Border Patrol in preventing illegal entry and drug smuggling (see Thalacker 1980, p. 79).

It is easy to dismiss artists such as Rios for "selling out." On the other hand, artists must survive, and one way is through sponsorship. The problem is that sponsorship starkly emphasizes the problem of the tension between the artist and society. In postrevolutionary societies, this problem expresses itself most often in the artist's pursuit of individualism and experimentation being regarded as a luxury and a danger by the state. In nonrevolutionary democratic societies, however, the problem emerges as the dilemma of the artist attempting to engage in socially committed art and concomitantly seeking sponsorship. Basically, there are only three possible solutions to the problem.

First, the artist can engage in self-censorship, not antagonizing the sponsors and saving the more socially committed art for another time and place. Thus, the great Mexican muralists were all invited to the United States in the early 1930s to paint murals. Orozco criticized aspects of the United States in his murals in Pomona, California, but in a symbolic and oblique way. Rivera painted his "Portrait of Detroit" in 1932–1933 using money provided by the Ford Motor Company. The mural contains no indictment of U.S. capitalism, but in the words of Myers (1956, 82) it is "a monumental glorification of industry."

Second, the artist can be somewhat subversive, accepting the sponsorship but seeking to include more obvious criticism somewhere in the painting's content. Thus Rivera, despite his caution in Detroit, was more forward in the more politically charged atmosphere of New York. In his mural at Rockefeller Center, he included a portrait of Lenin, an act of subversion that later led to the destruction of the entire mural (see Myers 1956, p. 83). A mural by Siqueiros, painted at the same time in Los Angeles, also was whitewashed and Siqueiros was required to leave the city prematurely. The mural directly criticized the treatment of Mexicans living in the United States (see Myers 1956, p. 119). Finally, as we have seen, the murals of some indigenous radical artists in the United States met a similar fate because of their critical, especially pro-communist, content.

Third, the artist can drop out of the race for sponsorship based on clear indications that when the state supports mural programs, its reasons are at odds with those of any radical artists working on them. This is Kelly's (1984, p. 25) advice. Writing of the British experience, he argues that the community arts movement

> allowed itself to be fashioned by its desire to seek funding, and by its willingness to ignore the price that was exacted for that funding—in the form of a progressive loss of control over the direction of the movement . . .

In Kelly's (1984, p. 97) words, the movement became "addicted to grant aid which was provided at all times in amounts and in ways which suited the funding agency." As a result, it ended up "no more revolutionary than the district nurse." What is the alternative? Kelly (1984, p. 125) proposes that community artists, muralists included, should reject the chimera of being "a salaried cultural revolutionary" and organize as independent workers. Flexible networks and alliances can allow for collective strength and for moving ahead as a genuinely oppositional force rather than the coopted one that it has become.

Funding is still the problem. Artists can find money for paint and tools (but not salaries) in ingenious ways. Barnett (1984, p. 185) points out that most Mexican murals in Los Angeles were funded through local donations. In Chicano Park, for example, local people sold their blood to buy brushes and paint (see Barnett 1984, p. 162). Local people in Chicago became "shareholders" in one mural, "buying" bricks at fifty cents each (see Barnett 1984, p. 353).

On the other hand, these examples seem to be exceptions to the rule, as is clear from Barnett's comprehensive review of community murals in the United States in the 1970s. Boston's mural program, Summerthing, was sponsored by the Mayor's Office of Cultural Affairs. In Los Angeles, Judy Baca engaged local youths in the painting of what is perhaps the longest mural in the world—13 feet high and one third of a mile long, and still unfinished in 1981 (see Rickey 1981)—using money from Los Angeles' Department of Recreation and Parks. Barnett (1984, p. 115) notes that most of the community murals were funded from such sources, particularly by the National Endowment for the Arts in the early 1970s and the Comprehensive Employment and Training Agency of the Department of Labor in the late 1970s. Both organizations provided money to "cool out" the ghetto, and the funds began to dry up when the inner city spawned fewer riots and less unrest.

In short, such funding had strings. It was given for social control—"cooling out" the ghetto, rehabilitating drug addicts (as with the muralists Los Artes Guadalupanos de Aztlan in Santa Fe, New Mexico; see Barnett 1984, p. 115), providing diversionary activities for potentially delinquent gang members (as with the funding of Judy Baca's "Great Wall of Los Angeles" [see Barnett 1984, p. 109], and many other murals in Los Angeles [see Simpson 1980, p. 522]). In many cases, such sponsors were consequently quite specific about what they expected of murals. In Philadelphia, the sponsors of Urban Outreach argued that political art had enough outlets and that the community murals sponsored by them must be apolitical (see Barnett 1984, p. 356). In Boston, the Mayor's Office of Cultural Affairs was very wary of socially conscious murals and instead supported "chic abstractions and supergraphics" (Barnett 1984, p. 97).

All of this seems to confirm Kelly's (1984) pessimistic conclusion that funding is the source of the depoliticization of the community arts movement. On the other hand, this conclusion may be overgeneralized. Community murals began in the United States in the late 1960s, one of the first being William Walker's "Wall of Respect" in Chicago in 1967. The first murals were by black artists like Walker. Mexicans followed quickly and within a decade, in Barnett's (1984, p. 166) estimation, they had produced more than 1,000 murals in Los Angeles alone. For ethnic minorities, then, these murals became a form of empowerment, a way of "raising people's social and political understanding" (Barnett 1984, p. 242). The content of many ethnic murals was often remarkably apolitical, even consensual, but their quantity and quality gave ethnic minorities a sense of pride and identity denied them in mainstream art, as in mainstream United States society generally.

Judy Baca in Los Angeles would undoubtedly agree. Despite the social control intentions of the Department of Recreation and Parks, working on a mural project that sought to chart the experiences of ethnic minorities in California provided her potentially delinquent young people with a unique opportunity: "it . . . gives them a sense of their history" (cited in Rickey 1981, p. 57).

It is possible to be euphoric about community arts, painting a picture that mirrors Kelly's pessimism. This is the sense that comes across partially from a reading of Barnett (1984) or Cockcroft, Weber, and Cockcroft (1977). It also is a sense that can be inspired by the proliferation of "nice pictures" of murals in books such as those of Barthelmeh's (1981 and 1982) approach. But euphoria begs the question of whether what is revolutionary in artistic terms is necessarily also revolutionary in political and social terms. Those who would like to believe that it can be, that, in Braden's (1978, p. 162) words, "a drawing, for instance, can change someone's relationship with their landlord," posit their faith on a rejection of the elitism of contemporary art. Art has become, as Pearson (1982, p. 101) puts it, artists' art, "art produced for other artists as the audience." It is a self-contained entity, an international language taught to and understood by the few and confined to the esoteric temples of galleries and museums. In such a situation, the act of breaking out of the cultural ghetto of "high art" becomes a radical act. Art is dissociated from society and politics; to put art back into the community is to reconnect it with political and social issues.

But art in the community need not break down the fence built around high culture. As Braden (1978, p. 161) notes, some mural artists see the wall merely as a larger easel. If this occurs, then the definition of radicalism is confined to an internal debate within the art profession. If radicalism is achieved simply by changing the location of the product, then the challenge enacted is one to the art world and not necessarily to the wider society. For example, Cork (1978, p. 10) is ecstatic in his praise of a mural by David Binnington and Desmond Rochfort painted under a motorway flyover in the Royal Oak area of London. The landscape is run-down, impersonal, "brutal," and "uncompromising"; "the alienation is numbing." Yet in the middle of this urban decay is the mural, which is "determined to offer a corrective to the incoherent dreariness elsewhere." It is abstract and modernist, but

the pleasure of finding a monumental mural executed with such demonstrable care, within an environment where caring is otherwise hard to find, is soon intensified by the equally welcome realisation that these paintings are not simply whimsical decorations 'brightening up' an oppressive locale.

Rather, they grow out of and rail against the dehumanized surroundings and their ultimate cause, industrial capitalism. The question is whether anyone other than Binnington, Rochfort, and Cork realizes the import of the mural. Despite noting the artists' attempts to consult local people, Cork reveals a great deal when he concludes that "whether or not local people approve of it, the mural is therefore part of the everyday fabric of life at Royal Oak." Thus the cat is let out of the bag. Community art, in Cork's estimation, makes art "a familiar landmark rather than a remote activity sealed off in special places reserved for privileged culture." Its challenge therefore is to the inhabitants of these special places rather than to the guardians of industrial capitalism or the managers of urban decay.

The practice of community arts is not necessarily revolutionary; on the other hand, it is not inherently counter-revolutionary. Such generalizations are too broad to be valid. At the same time, some less grand generalizations can be made. Officially sponsored community arts are often intended by their sponsors to be apolitical and consensual. Thus obstacles are put in the way of any artist attempting to make a radical, even a socially aware, statement through art. Although some artists break through these obstacles, leading to disproportionate attention to and controversy over their art, this usually is not the case. The control mechanisms, articulated and otherwise, work, not least because such schemes often attract artists orbiting in the same universe of discourse as the sponsors.

However, it should not be concluded that community art deriving from outside the channels of state sponsorship is necessarily more radical. Ley and Cybriwsky (1974, p. 494) reach this conclusion, seeing the graffiti of urban teenagers as a subconscious challenge to mainstream U.S. society.

> Climbing mountains, descending to the ocean depths, landing astronauts on the moon who leave behind their own territorial marker, colonial adventures, riding the freeway, possessing a home on a large lot—middle-income Americans have ample opportunity to sublimate their territorial needs, but many of these options are closed to the inner city dweller. For him [*sic*], spatial mastery is often possible only in the realms of the phantasmagorical.

In a similar vein, Romotsky and Romotsky (1976, p. 654) argue in obscure jargon that there is much more psychological and political import in graffiti than meets the untrained eye.

> The street can be seen as synergistic because of the expansive potential in aesthetic experience, but mostly because the public room called a street is public, populous and therefore popular.

But such decidedly political interpretations are not at the forefront of the conscious motivation of the graffiti artists who adorn the subway trains of New York. For them, the emphasis is on "making your name sing" (Castleman 1982, p. 53), on style. The "writers" of New York may have their own shared norms and values (and vocabulary; see Cooper and Chalfant 1984, p. 27), but their challenge is not politically motivated. As members of a coherent subculture, they were inherently no more or less challenging to the social and political structures of the United States in the 1970s than rock and roll was in the previous two decades.

The same conclusion may be reached about much of the "head art" of groups such as the Los Angeles Fine Arts Squad (see Schmidt-Brummer 1982; Schmidt-Brummer and Lee 1973; Greenberg, Smyth, and Teacher 1977), or the murals by various artists in the "alternative community" of Venice, California (see Schmidt-Brummer 1973). With their roots in the hippie culture of the 1960s, such murals frequently criticized the established order, often in a witty way. But, like that wider culture, this art could not easily drop out of mainstream U.S. society. The art was often good and therefore open to commercialization. In this way the sting was removed quickly from the tail of these "alternative" murals. Why that

should have occurred so easily is explained by Barnett (1984, p. 239); head art "never had the kind of deeply rooted base in a neighborhood that was common with community murals." The same point is put more generally and forcefully by Sommer (1975, pp. 3–4):

> Many white artists are intensely concerned with pollution, population control and the other themes of the ecology movement, yet few street murals reflect ecological concerns. White artists lack a definable geographic community requiring this kind of art, so they have turned their attention to an art game played with collectors, critics, patrons and dealers. The satirical put-downs, frivolity and faddism of modern art movements can be viewed as a response to a lack of community.

Such noncommunity-based art only manages, in Barnett's (1984, p. 458) words, to "invite us to shake our heads at the folly of modern life and go on pursuing it."

In head art the radicalism was one of form only. But art that also is politically radical—that is, connected to a movement that is itself politically threatening—faces only two options in relation to sponsorship: either to apply knowing that refusal is almost inevitable, or not to apply for precisely that same reason.

For republican muralists in Northern Ireland, therefore, the question of state sponsorship does not arise. They do not seek, nor do they get, such funding. Instead, murals are produced as a result of borrowing paint, providing free labor, and getting some backing from sympathetic groups such as Sinn Féin.

As far as the state is concerned, there has been little backing for community muralists; again, the result is that tension between sponsorship and independence rarely arises. Tensions rarely emerged even during the most major project to date—the state-sponsored community mural programme in Belfast between 1977 and 1981. Political radicalism is not a keynote of the art establishment in Northern Ireland, and consequently it is not held up as an ideal to the art students who painted the community murals. On the contrary, their training to be "dispassionate commentators" inspires a separation of art and politics, whereby *radical* is seen as a word relating only to art fashions, and the students become "guerrilla muralists." However, unlike the Ramona Parra mural brigades in Chile, they were emissaries of the establishment, not of the radical opposition to it.

Loyalist muralists, with their long tradition in Northern Ireland, present a third variant on sponsorship. At no time have loyalist muralists, despite their close organizational ties with state institutions especially before the demise of the devolved government and parliament in 1972, received state funding.[3] Their murals, like those of the republicans, have been funded in the most ad hoc of ways. At the same time it must be stressed that their ideological affinity with the state has allowed loyalist muralists a legitimacy that could be subsumed under the general notion of sponsorship. The link was not direct nor material, but in a situation in which murals were ritualized, quasi-state memorials, there was no tension between state and muralist. After 1972 loyalists had to rely increasingly on the community rather than the state, as well as aspiring

to an idealized state that cannot exist while British Direct Rule persists. State ideological sponsorship no longer is the norm, and a tension has emerged, most notably in terms of the oppositionalism inherent in the more militaristic of recent loyalist murals. The opposition is not one to the state itself, however, but to the real state for not living up the image of the ideal state.

In another age it might have been possible to imagine a community murals program in Northern Ireland happily funding the production of loyalist murals, but not of republican ones. But by the time the fashion of community murals emerged, the disjunction between loyalism and the state had occurred. State sponsorship was confined, for the most part, to a series of bland murals, reflecting in their own small way a different ideological affinity, that between the state and the art establishment to have nothing to do with "extremism."

WHY MURALS?

The "extremists" turned to alternate channels because they had not got access to state channels of communication. Yet, the question that needs to be answered is why they chose mural painting as the main medium.

In other societies, murals have been rejected by politically articulate groups as a worthwhile form of propaganda. Despite their commitment to other forms of publicly accessible art—posters and vallas[4]—the Cubans, in Kunzle's (1975, p. 100) words, rejected murals as

> too realistic, heavy and rhetorical in style and too expensive and permanent in medium to serve as a model for a Cuba which demands flexibility and mobility, as well as greater ideological control than the Mexicans were ever subjected to.

In this way the Cubans have followed in the footsteps of the Soviet Revolution that also rejected murals as a worthwhile form of propaganda. Berger (1969, quoted in Stermer 1970, pp. xxvii) justifies the Soviet decision in the following terms.

> Oil painting, sculpture and in most cases mural painting do not as media lend themselves to propaganda. Their facture suggests too great a degree

of permanence. Furthermore, they are functionally inefficient media for propaganda purposes. A painting or a statue can only be in one place at one time, seen by a very limited number of people. The possible modern media for propaganda are film, the ideogrammatic (not naturalistic) poster, the booklet, certain forms of theatre, the song and declamatory poetry.

The problem of such a finalistic conclusion is that it presumes that mass mobilization only can be achieved through mass media. There are alternative possibilities, not least that mass mobilizations can be built up through the accretion of mini-mobilizations. In this case, media with more localized impact have a crucial role to play. For example, Bassets (1983, p. 195) notes that the Communist Party in Spain developed various methods of "clandestine communication" in resistance to Franco's dictatorship. They included the practice in Catalonia of painting single letter slogans: A (for amnesty), L (for liberty), and P (for protest). Often no one knew what these letters meant except the Communist Party militants themselves. In other words, the main function of this small-scale, low-tech propaganda was to present a badge of identity, a label of legitimacy to the members of the resistance themselves. Even if the slogans did not persuade or convert any one outside the movement, they acted as solidarity for members.

In a situation in which open dictatorship is not the form of government, such propaganda can reach grander levels. As the Franco regime weakened, the Basques found it possible to be more open about propaganda. First graffiti became widespread and then large numbers of colorful and original murals emerged (see Departamento Cultural Vizcaina 1986). Chaffee (1988, p. 547) argues that the Basque case proves that graffiti and murals provide

> an easily accessible communication medium open to grass roots organisations and individuals to challenge the dominant control that dictatorships have over the media and the expression of ideas.

Moreover, when the Franco era ended the need to break out of years of imposed cultural silence, as well as the fact that the centrally controlled mass media of the new democratic state failed to provide a channel for this release, meant that the mural tradition grew rather than waned. As a result, murals became an effective form of political mobilization, managing not only to enhance group cohesion, but also to persuade or convert others to the cause. The surest sign of their effectiveness is the existence of right wing, anti-ETA murals and slogans throughout the Basque country (see Chaffee 1988, pp. 559–60).

The parallels with Northern Ireland are striking. The republican movement in the early 1980s moved from a long period of containment into one of confidence and mass mobilization. Culture became one pillar of the movement's self-definition, and cultural expression—in language, music, and mural painting—became a key element in the newfound confidence. Unionism moved from its traditional position of political sureness to one of uncertainty. Loyalist murals were never state murals, although done with the unionist state's imprimatur. With British control of the state the murals became increasingly the propaganda arm of those unionists most determined to take a militaristic way out of political confusion.

For both loyalists and republicans, murals are an important form of political mobilization, not least at the local level. It must be remembered that not everyone in a nationalist or unionist community shares the aspirations and ideology of republicanism or loyalism, respectively. Murals became crucial in two ways: providing a sense of cohesion to the "converted" and acting as a potential source of "conversion" of others. In both senses, although highly immobile and localized, their role in the mass mobilization of both republicans and loyalists is beyond question.

Accordingly, murals are not dismissed as easily as Berger would suggest. Like any medium of political mobilization, their effectiveness depends on circumstances. In this respect murals are similar to other such media. For example, speaking of posters, Sontag (1970, p. xii) concludes

> Maxi-mobilization is a realistically feasible goal when posters are the vehicle of a ruling political doctrine. Insurgent or revolutionary posters aim, more modestly, at a mini-mobilization of opinion against the prevailing official line.

The measure of such revolutionary art, paraphrasing a concept used by Gramsci, is the extent to which it is "organic" to the political movement concerned. Based on this criterion, Kelly (1984, p. 115) rejects murals sponsored by the Greater London Council in the early 1980s, although the themes were often radical.

> Such murals do not provide a focal point for a group, nor an emblem for a community. They simply oppress people. They are ideological advertisements rendered more permanent than any capitalists would dare render their advertisements, and they oppress in precisely the same way as any other advertisement.

Despite the radical content, the "sub-text" of such murals "is a celebration of the domination of the local state over its subjects."[5]

There is, then, a world of difference between such murals and those of the Mexican artists of the 1920s. Siqueiros's choice of mural painting as a medium was radical artistically. As he said in his "Declaration of Social, Political and Aesthetic Principles," written in 1922, (Siqueiros 1975, p. 25)

We repudiate so-called easel painting and every

kind of art favoured by ultra-intellectual circles, because it is aristocratic, and we praise monumental art in all its forms, because it is public property.

In almost identical terms, Orozco (quoted in Franco 1970, p. 157) was committed to the mural because

> it cannot be made a matter of private gain; it cannot be hidden away for the benefit of a certain privileged few. It is for the people.

Similarly, Leger in France (quoted in Gaudibert 1983, p. 185) was influenced by the Mexican experiment, and thus saw murals as a break "with the post-Renaissance individualism of intimist painting destined for private appropriation."

But form and location alone are not enough to make this art genuinely revolutionary. Siqueiros and Orozco were part of a revolutionary movement, the former more directly than the latter. Leger's murals, like himself, were part of the socialist ferment of France in the 1930s. Thus it was the organic nature of the murals, their intimate relationship to a political upsurge, that made them revolutionary art.

Ireland is not Mexico. The loyalist and republican murals, unlike those sponsored by the state, are organically connected to political movements. Neither movement is in control of the state, although each has its aspirations for the kind of state it desires. Murals are part of the process of political definition; their function is mobilization. That mobilization takes place at the local level but is no less important for that. After all, although also fought out at the society and international levels, it is at the local level that the battle for state legitimacy is waged daily. In the midst of that battle, murals are not just folk artifacts but a crucial factor in the politicization of the community. Politically articulate murals simultaneously become expressions of and creators of community solidarity. Although it would be too far-fetched to argue that the propaganda war is won or lost at the local level, there can be no denying the role the murals play as crucial weapons in that war.

Notes

CHAPTER 1. TRIUMPH AND CONFUSION: LOYALIST WALL MURALS

1. A similar "Roman emperor" style statue of King William exists in Hull. For a photograph see *Belfast Telegraph,* 24 August 1987, on the occasion of the undertaking of repairs to the statue costing forty thousand pounds.

2. *Belfast Telegraph,* 8 August 1987. In a similar vein, note Prime Minister Terence O'Neill's remark in 1969: "If you treat Roman Catholics with due consideration and kindness, they will live like Protestants, in spite of the authoritative nature of their church" (quoted in Farrell 1980, p. 256).

3. *Crack* is slang for good conversation, fun, and all round enjoyment. For an incisive but unsympathetic consideration of the Twelfth as crack, see Belfrage 1987, pp. 132–61.

4. Unless otherwise noted, all streets and areas mentioned in relation to specific murals, arches, and so on are in Belfast.

5. It was known for these bands to be at the center of trouble around the Twelfth. Thus in 1935 one band from Glasgow, the Billy Boys, was reprimanded by a Glasgow newspaper after their playing of party tunes at a wake led to an incident in which two more unionists died. "Why do the authorities permit a party of people to march behind a band carrying a wreath to the home of a man who had been shot the night before? Of course, the wreath was a sincere tribute to the dead, but the manner of its delivery cannot be called anything but an ostentatious piece of provocation for the living" (*Glasgow Herald,* 14 July 1935; quoted in Munck and Rolston 1987, p. 50).

6. Fred Heatley, a local historian and author, remembers a mural in Rowan Street around 1945 or 1946. Dedicated to "our three glorious heroes," it contained portraits of Churchill, Roosevelt, and Stalin.

7. Lundy was the traitor who threatened to surrender Derry to the blockading Williamite forces, but he was thwarted by apprentice boys who closed the city gates. The date of this event, 18 December, is still celebrated annually in Derry by burning a large effigy of Lundy; see Bell 1986a.

8. In 1969 this mural was still in good enough condition to be photographed for the *Sunday Times'* color magazine, 23 March 1969.

9. In this redevelopment, a classic slogan extant in Tigers Bay throughout the decade disappeared: "We shall not forsake the blue skies of freedom for the grey mists of an Irish republic."

10. Jenkins (1982, pp. 35–37) discusses the importance of the word *Kai* to the teenage boys of Rathcoole. He suggests several possible origins for the word, but does not refer to the slogan "Kill all Irish."

11. Many loyalists protested loudly against the republican practice in the 1980s of erecting street signs in Belfast and elsewhere translating the street name into Irish. At the same time, they attempted to copy the practice. Not having the specific identity of language to publicize, their signs were only loyalist in terms of the person after whom the street was renamed—Mark Street after Mark Bacon from Tigers Bay who died from stab wounds in a sectarian brawl over the Twelfth weekend in 1986 (see photograph in *Belfast Telegraph,* 23 September 1986), or Bingham Road (Ballysillan Road), named after a leading UVF man killed by the IRA in 1987.

12. Ironically, many of the flags carried by unionists on the Twelfth marches in the 1980s were made by a Dublin firm, Prospect Design. "We will make any flag we get an order for," said Ken Kearns of the family firm (see *Sunday Tribune,* 1 June 1986).

13. On the occasion of the visit of King Juan Carlos of Spain to Britain, the BBC News at 6 p.m. (23 April 1986) showed some black and white footage of Gibraltar in 1969, the year Franco closed the border to Spain. Included was a brief shot of an exterior wall mural in Gibraltar, consisting solely of a Union Jack and the words "The Symbol of Freedom."

14. For a critical assessment of the origins and progress of the Anglo-Irish Agreement, see Rolston 1987.

CHAPTER 2. "COOLING OUT THE COMMUNITY"? BELFAST'S COMMUNITY MURAL PROGRAM

1. The most notable intervention of poets and playwrights in the Irish political scene recently has been that of the Field Day Theatre Company in a series of pamphlets (see Field Day Theatre Company 1986, in which the first six of these pamphlets were republished together in book form). This political intervention has been attacked by some critics (see Longley 1984) but also has been defended by others (see McMinn 1985).

2. Jack Pakenham, a Belfast-based artist who also takes up themes relating to the "troubles" in his work, makes the same point about artistic detachment in much more emotive terms; he sees the necessity not merely of distancing art from the troubles but of using art to reject them.

> In my paintings over the past three years I have returned to depicting local themes. I still feel the need to highlight the hypocrisy, the bigotry, the perverted logic of our poor insane Ulster, where psychopaths from both sides have decided that if I do not agree with them and their plans for my future, they will cripple me or blind me or bomb me into submission. It seems to me we are getting closer and closer to a Fascist state, where people are not going to be allowed to have individual opinions, where opposition has to be eliminated, where words such as "Compromise," "Reconciliation" just do not exist. My paintings are my protest, my accusing and condemning finger. (Arts Council Gallery Exhibition Information, February 1987)

3. A report by the Fair Employment Agency in 1986 revealed that of more than 60 attendants employed by the Ulster Museum, only 8 percent were Catholics. See Fair Employment Agency 1986.

4. On the record of the councils in relation to community services, see Rolston 1985.

5. Unless stated otherwise, subsequent quotations are from written reports by the mural artists to their employers or the transcript of a taped interview with Ray and Yvonne McCullough conducted by the author.

6. Postcards of some of these murals were produced and sold by the Arts Council of Northern Ireland.

7. For more information about this mural scheme, as well as a photograph of one of the "Better Belfast" murals, see *Irish News*, 24 August 1988.

CHAPTER 3. ART AS A WEAPON: REPUBLICAN MURALS

1. "We may make mistakes in the beginning and shoot the wrong people; but bloodshed is a cleansing and a sanctifying thing." Patrick Pearse, *The Coming Revolution*, cited in Shaw 1972, p. 125.

2. On the arrangement of Irish dance music to suit the more middle class and unionist tastes of listeners to BBC Radio Ulster, see Cathcart 1985, p. 98.

3. The corollary of this is that partition served to depoliticize nationalist culture in the South.

4. The emblem of *An Phoblacht/Republican News*, the weekly newspaper of the republican movement, is a harp with the accompanying slogan, "It is new-strung and shall be heard."

5. Unless specified otherwise, all streets and areas mentioned in relation to specific murals are in Belfast.

6. For a comprehensive survey of the involvement of the Northern Ireland Office in such propaganda, see Loftus 1980b.

7. Rossville Flats in Derry also had a crude mural, a life-size silhouette of an RUC man swilling beer. For a photograph, see Carson 1976, p. 89.

8. For a sympathetic account of the compound system, see Crawford 1979. The Gardiner Report was published in 1975.

9. Such political art by prisoners is common elsewhere. For example, Dorfmann (1983, p. 210) notes that in Chile under Pinochet "culture has become essential in the con-

centration camps. Political prisoners have discovered the value and dignity that art confers on them." Bassets (1983, p. 197) says of Spain under Franco: "The first area of clandestinity after the republican defeat was undoubtedly the prison system."

10. Criminalization occurred in two phases. Firstly, all prisoners convicted of offenses committed after April 1976 were sent to the H Blocks, and all those convicted of offenses committed before that date continued to be sent to the compounds. By 1979 all sentenced prisoners were sent to the H Blocks, regardless of when their offence occurred.

11. Later some prison officers began to study Irish to be able to understand prisoners who speak to each other in Irish. See *Irish News*, 13 February 1987.

12. Bobby Sands's (1983, p. 53) own account of learning Irish is similar to that of Joseph Maguire. "The teacher was at the far end of the wing. He began to shout the lessons at the top of his voice from behind his heavy steel door, asking questions, spelling out words and phrases, while the willing pupils scratched and scribbled them upon the dirty mutilated walls. It was a rough and rugged way of teaching but it worked, and everyone endeavoured to speak what they learned all the time until the words and phrases became so common that they were used instinctively."

13. For the most comprehensive account of both hunger strikes, see Beresford 1987.

14. For a comprehensive introduction to this and other aspects of emergency law in Northern Ireland, see Hillyard 1983.

15. The Starry Plough was the flag of James Connolly's Irish Citizen Army. Currently it has seven white stars on a blue background, although originally it had yellow stars on a green background. For the story of this color transformation, see Hayes-McCoy 1979, 217–18.

16. The Fianna are the youth section of the republican movement. Their flag consists of an orange sunburst on a yellow background.

17. During the 1987 General Election in which Gerry Adams was re-elected MP for the area, this mural was regrettably replaced by a poorly painted quasi-mural that merely stated in large letters: "Freedom, Justice and Peace."

18. Photographs of both McCartan's harmless graffito and funeral appear in *National Geographic* 159, no. 4 (April 1981): pp. 496–97.

19. Sands was serving a determinate sentence. Had it not been for the outcome of the hunger strike, he would have been released before this mural was painted.

20. It is clear from the article within the same issue of *Soldier*, "Carry on up the Creggan", by Bill Moore that this was not the only mural in the British army base on Derry's walls. However, it was the cover photograph that caused dissension, specifically its attribution to the Green Howards. In a subsequent edition of *Soldier*, 11 July 1988, Sergeant J. Callaghan of the Anglian Regiment (also known as the Vikings) pointed out that his regiment had originally painted the mural, along with the slogan "Oglaigh na h-Vikings." An accompanying photograph provided by him proved the point.

CHAPTER 4. POLITICAL MURALS: INTERNATIONAL PERSPECTIVES

1. For photographs of the murals of another socialist

revolution, that of Mozambique, see Sachs 1984. Popular revolutions other than socialist inspired ones also have led to outbursts of mural painting; see, for example Cockcroft's (1981) account of murals in contemporary Iran.

2. "Ordinary Nicaraguans" included women muralists. For the work of two, Hilda Vogl Garcia and Julia Aguirre, see La Duke 1985, p. 25–28.

3. As recounted in chapter 1, the oldest extant loyalist mural in Northern Ireland was painted by Bobby Jackson and his father. When the area was redeveloped in the 1970s, the wall on which the mural was painted was demolished with precision and re-assembled a short distance away among new housing. At that point Jackson retouched the mural. The Northern Ireland Housing Executive paid an unspecified amount of money to resite this "historic monument," something they never could be envisaged doing if the mural in question were republican.

4. Vallas are the Cuban equivalent of large commercial advertisements. The sections hung together to produce the overall political image, however, are silk-screened.

5. In this regard the murals of Ray Walker are unique, particularly his celebration of ethnic diversity in Chicksand Street and his memorial to anti-fascist action in the 1930s in Cable Street, both in East London. The murals present all the signs of growing out of the politics and culture of the area rather than being imposed from without. See Ray Walker Memorial Committee 1985.

References

Adamson, I. 1974; rpt. 1986. *The Cruthin*. Belfast: Pretani Press.

Adamson, I. 1979. *Bangor, Light of the World*. Belfast: Pretani Press.

Adare, I. 1986. "Who Needs Off-White Concrete Towers?" *Circa* 26, Education Supplement Part 3, pp. 35–37.

As Paredes Na Revolucao. 1978. Lisboa: Mil Dias Editora.

Barnett, A. 1984. *Community Murals: the People's Art*. London: Cornwall Books.

Barthelmeh, V. 1981. *Kunst an der Wand*, Frankfurt am Main: Verlag Kieter Fricke.

Barthelmeh, V. 1982. *Street Murals*. Harmondsworth: Penguin.

Bassets, L. 1983. "Clandestine Communications: Notes on the Press and Propaganda of the Anti-Franco Resistance, 1939–1975." In *Communication and Class Struggle, volume 2. Liberation, Socialism*. ed. A. Mattelart and S. Siegelaub, pp. 192–200. New York/Bagnolet: International General/International Mass Media Research Center.

Belfast Bulletin 11. 1985. *Supergrasses*. Belfast: Workers' Research Unit.

Belfrage, S. 1987. *The Crack: A Belfast Year*. London: Andre Deutsch.

Bell, D. 1986(a). "The Traitor Within the Gates." *New Society* 3 (January).

Bell, D. 1986(b). "Acts of Union: Youth Subculture and Ethnic Identity amongst Protestants in Northern Ireland." Unpublished paper to Sociological Association of Ireland Annual Conference, Dublin.

Benjamin, W. 1982. "The Author as Producer". In *Modern Art and Modernism: A Critical Anthology*, ed.

F. Frascina and C. Harrison, pp. 213–16. London: Harper and Row.

Beresford, D. 1987. *Ten Men Dead*. London: Grafton Books.

Berger, J. 1972. *Ways of Seeing*. London-Harmondsworth: BBC Publications-Penguin.

Berman, D.; Lalor, S.; and Torode, B. 1983. "The Theology of the IRA." *Studies* 72:2 (Summer): pp. 137–44.

Berman, G. 1977. "The Walls of Harlem." *Arts Magazine* 52: pp. 122–26.

Braden, S. 1978. *Artists and People*, London: Routledge and Kegan Paul.

Breslin, S. 1972. "By their Walls you shall Know them." *Aquarius* 5: pp. 66–71.

Buckley, A. 1986. "Drums and Symbols." *The Guardian* 5 September.

Carson, W. 1976. *Derry Through the Lens*. Donegal: Donegal Democrat.

Castleman, C. 1982. *Getting Up: Subway Grafitti in New York*. Cambridge: MIT Press.

Cathcart, R. 1985. *The Most Contrary Region: The BBC in Northern Ireland 1924–1984*. Belfast: Appletree Press.

Catto, M. 1977. "Notes from a Small War: Art and the Troubles." In *Art in Ulster*, vol. 2, M. Catto, pp. 125–44. Belfast: Blackstaff Press.

Chaffee, L. 1988. "Social Conflict and Alternative Mass Communications: Public Art and Politics in the Service of Spanish-Basque Nationalism." *European Journal of Political Research* 16: pp. 545–72.

Cockcroft, E. 1981. "Post-Shah Art." *Art in America* 69: pp. 26–29.

Cockcroft, E.; Weber, J.; and Cockcroft, J. 1977. *To-*

ward a People's Art: the Contemporary Mural Movement. New York: E. P. Dutton and Co.

Collins, T. 1983. *The Centre Cannot Hold.* Dublin and Belfast: Bookworks.

Collins, T. 1986. *The Irish Hunger Strike.* Dublin and Belfast: White Island Books.

Committee for Withdrawal from Ireland. 1980. *Ireland: Voices for Withdrawal.* London.

Constantine, M., and Fern, A. eds. 1974. *Revolutionary Soviet Film Posters.* Baltimore: Johns Hopkins University Press.

Coogan, T. P. 1980. *On the Blanket.* Dublin: Ward River Press.

Cooper, G., and Sargent, D. 1979. *Painting the Town.* Oxford: Phaidon.

Cooper, M., and Chalfant, H. 1984. *Subway Art.* London: Thames and Hudson.

Cope, P. 1987. "Nicaragua: a Different Kind of Democracy." In *Strong Voices: Culture and Democracy in Chile and Nicaragua,* pp. 11–14. West Bromwich: Another Standard.

Cork, R. 1978. "The Royal Oak Murals." *Art Monthly* 15: pp. 10–11.

Crawford, C. 1979. "Long Kesh: an Alternative Perspective." Unpublished M.Sc. thesis, Cranfield Institute of Technology.

Curtis, L. 1982. *They Shoot Children: the Use of Rubber and Plastic Bullets in the North of Ireland.* London: Information on Ireland.

Curtis, L. 1984. *Ireland: the Propaganda War.* London: Pluto Press.

De Bure, G. 1981. *Des Murs Dans La Ville.* Paris: L'Equerre.

Departamento Cultural Vizcaina. 1986. *Expresion Mural.* Pais Vasco, Spain.

Departamento de Propaganda y Educacion del FSLN. 1981. *El Mural,* Managua, Nicaragua.

Devlin, B. 1985. *An Interlude with Seagulls.* London: Information on Ireland.

Devlin, P. 1981. *Yes, We Have No Bananas.* Belfast: Blackstaff Press.

Dillon, M. and Lehane, D. 1973. *Political Murder in Northern Ireland.* Harmondsworth: Penguin.

Dorfmann, A. 1983. "The Invisible Chile: Three Years of Cultural Resistance." In *Communication and Class Struggle, volume 2. Liberation, Socialism,* ed. A. Mattelart and S. Siegelaub, pp. 207–10. New York/Bagnelot: International General/International Mass Media Research Centre.

(Ellis, B.) 1985. *Victims and Survivors: the Work of Brendan Ellis.* Exhibition catalog. Belfast: Art and Research Exchange/Arts Council of Northern Ireland.

Fair Employment Agency. 1986. *Report of an Investigation under Section 12 of the Fair Employment (Northern Ireland) Act into the Ulster Museum.* Belfast: Fair Employment Agency.

Farrell, M. 1980. *Northern Ireland: The Orange State.* London: Pluto Press.

Field Day Theatre Company. 1986. *Ireland's Field Day.* London: Hutchinson.

Fitzpatrick, J. 1983. *The Silver Arm.* Dundalk: De Danaan Press.

Franco, J. 1970. *The Modern Culture of Latin America, Society and the Artist.* Baltimore: Penguin Books.

Fraser, S. E. 1977. *One Hundred Great Chinese Posters.* New York: Images Graphiques.

Gardiner Report. 1975. *Measures to Deal with Terrorism in Northern Ireland.* London: HMSO, Cmnd. 5847.

Gaudibert, P. 1983. "The Popular Front and the Arts." In *Communication and Class Struggle, volume 2. Liberation, Socialism,* ed. A. Mattelart and S. Siegelaub, pp. 182–89. New York/Bagnelot: International General/International Mass Media Research Centre.

Gibbon, P. 1975. *The Origins of Ulster Unionism.* Manchester: Manchester University Press.

Grasskamp, W., and Kottek, A. 1982. "Wandmalerei in Portugal." *Kunstforum International* 50: pp. 88–97.

Gray, C. 1962. *The Russian Experiment in Art, 1863–1922.* London: Thames and Hudson.

Greenberg, D.; Smyth, K.; and Teacher, S. 1977. *Megamurals and Supergraphics: Big Art.* Philadelphia: Running Press.

Grieb, K. 1984. "The Writing on the Walls: Grafitti as Government Propaganda in Mexico." *Journal of Popular Culture* 18: pp. 78–91.

Hayes-McCoy, G. A. 1979. *A History of Irish Flags from Earliest Times.* Dublin: Academy Press.

Hillyard, P. 1983. "Law and Order." In *Northern Ireland: Background to the Conflict,* ed. J. Darby, pp. 32–60. Belfast: Appletree Press.

Information on Ireland. 1982. *Cormac Strikes Back.* London: Information on Ireland.

Isles, K. S., and Cuthbert, N. 1957. *An Economic Survey of Northern Ireland.* Belfast: HMSO.

Janke, P. 1983. *Guerrilla and Terrorist Organisations: A World Directory and Bibliography.* Brighton: Harvester Press.

Jenkins, R. 1982. *Hightown Rules: Growing Up in a*

Belfast Housing Estate. Leicester: National Youth Bureau.

Johnston, E. 1970. "Folk Art in Ulster." *Architectural Review*: pp. 205–6.

Kearney, R. 1978. "Myth and Terror." *The Crane Bag*. 2, part 2, pp. 125–39.

Kelly, O. 1984. *Community, Art and the State: Storming the Citadels*. London: Comedia.

Killen, J. 1986. *John Bull's Famous Circus*. Dublin: O'Brien Press.

(Kindness, J. and Davies, A.) 1985. *Exploding Myths*. Exhibition catalog. Derry: Orchard Gallery.

Kitson, F. 1971. *Low Intensity Operations*. London: Faber and Faber.

Kunzle, D. 1975. "Public Graphics in Cuba." *Latin American Perspectives* 2.

Kunzle, D. 1978. "Art and the New Chile: Mural, Poster and Comic Book in a Revolutionary Process." In *Art and Architecture in the Service of Politics*, ed. H. Millon and L. Nochlin, pp. 356–81. Cambridge: MIT Press.

La Duke, B. 1984(a). "Nicaragua 1984: the Rifle and Paintbrush Coexist." *Journal of Popular Culture* 18, no. 2: pp. 43–56.

La Duke, B. 1984(b). "Women, Art and Culture in the New Grenada." *Latin American Perspectives* 12: pp. 37–52.

La Duke, B. 1985. *Companeras: Women, Art and Social Change in Latin America*. San Francisco: City Lights Books.

Lambert, G. 1983. "A Matrix of Contemporary Irish Visual Art." In *Ireland and the Arts*. ed. T. P. Coogan, pp. 198–205. London: Namara Press.

Ley, D., and Cybriwsky, R. 1974. "Urban Grafitti as Territorial Markers." *Annals of the Association of American Geographers* 64: pp. 491–505.

Loftus, B. 1977. "Will the Real King Billy Please Stand Up?" *Fortnight* 142: pp. 8–9.

Loftus, B. 1980(a). "Wall-Painting in Northern Ireland: An Occasion for Celebration?" Belfast: Unpublished paper.

Loftus, B. 1980(b). "Images for Sale: Government and Security Advertising in Northern Ireland 1969–1978." *Oxford Art Journal* October, pp. 70–80.

Longley, E. 1984. "More Martyrs to Abstraction." *Fortnight* 206: pp. 18, 20.

Loudan, J. "The Origin of the Big Drum." *Belfast Telegraph*, 7 July 1961.

Macardle, D. n.d. *Tragedies of Kerry*. Dublin: Irish Book Bureau.

McGuffin, J. 1973. *Internment*. Tralee: Anvil Books.

McKinzie, R. 1972. *The New Deal for Artists*. Princeton: Princeton University Press.

McLennan, A. 1985. "Walking Backward into the Future." *Circa* 25, Education Supplement Part 2, pp. 19–21.

McMinn, J. 1985. "In Defence of Field Day: Talking among the Ruins." *Fortnight* 224: 19–20.

McWilliams, J. 1982. "Violence and Painting in Northern Ireland." *Circa* May/June: p. 7.

Messenger, C. 1985. *Northern Ireland: The Troubles*. Twickenham: Hamlyn.

Miller, D. 1978. *Queen's Rebels*. Dublin: Gill and Macmillan.

Munck, R., and Rolston, B. 1987. *Belfast in the Thirties: An Oral History*. Belfast: Blackstaff Press.

Myers, B. 1956. *Mexican Painting in Our Time*. New York: Oxford University Press.

Nairn, T. 1977. *The Break-up of Britain*. London: New Left Books.

Nelson, S. 1984. *Ulster's Uncertain Defenders*. Belfast: Appletree Press.

Nissen, C. 1976. "Wandbilder im Kampf der Portugiesischen Kommunistischen Partei." *Bildende Kunst* 24: pp. 23–26.

O'Dowd, L. 1980. "Regional Policy." In *Northern Ireland: Between Civil Rights and Civil War*, L. O'Dowd, B. Rolston, and M. Tomlinson. London: CSE Books.

O'Dowd, L.; Rolston, B.; and Tomlinson, M. 1982. "From Labour to the Tories: The Ideology of Containment in Northern Ireland." *Capital and Class* 18: pp. 72–90.

Pearson, N. 1982. *The State and the Visual Arts*. Milton Keynes: Open University Press.

Ray Walker Memorial Committee. 1985. *Ray Walker*. London: Coracle Press.

Rees, M. 1985. *Northern Ireland: A Personal Perspective*. London: Methuen.

Rickey, C. 1981. "The Writing on the Wall." *Art in America*, May, pp. 54–57.

Roche, D. 1984. "The Political Consequences of a Changing Pattern of Violence." *Fortnight* 207, pp. 4–7.

Rodriguez, N. M. 1974. "The Archetypal Vision: a Marxist and Jungian Study of Mural Art." Ph.D. thesis, University College Los Angeles.

Rolston, B. 1980. "Community Politics." In *Northern Ireland: Between Civil Rights and Civil War*, L.

O'Dowd, B. Rolston, and M. Tomlinson, pp. 148–77. London: CSE Books.

Rolston, B. 1985. "Community Services in Northern Ireland: The Last Ten Years." *Critical Social Policy* 14: pp. 83–92.

Rolston, B. 1987. "Alienation or Political Awareness? The Battle for the Hearts and Minds of Northern Nationalists." In *Beyond the Rhetoric: Politics, the Economy and Social Policy in Northern Ireland*, P. Teague, ed., pp. 58–80. London: Lawrence and Wishart.

Rolston, B., and Tomlinson, M. 1986. "Long-term Imprisonment in Northern Ireland: Psychological or Political Survival?" In *The Expansion of European Prison Systems*, B. Rolston and M. Tomlinson, eds., pp. 162–83. Working Papers in European Criminology number 7. Belfast: European Group for the Study of Deviance and Social Control.

Rolston, B. and Tomlinson, M. 1988. " 'The Challenge Within': Prisons and Propaganda in Northern Ireland." In M. Tomlinson, T. Varley, and C. McCullagh, eds., pp. 167–92. Belfast: Sociological Association of Ireland.

Romotsky, J., and Romotsky, S. 1976. "L.A. Human Scale: Street Art of Los Angeles." *Journal of Popular Culture* 10, part 3, pp. 653–63.

Sachs, A. 1984. *Imagens de Uma Revolucao: Os Murais de Maputo*. Maputo: DNPP-MINFO.

Sands, B. 1981. *The Writings of Bobby Sands*. Dublin: Sinn Féin Prisoner of War Department.

Sands, B. 1983. *One Day in My Life*. London: Pluto Press.

Schmidt-Brummer, H. 1973. *Venice, California: An Urban Fantasy,* New York: Grossman.

Schmidt-Brummer, H. 1982. *Wandmalerei: Zwischen Reklamakunst, Phantasie und Protest*. Köln: Du Mont Buchverlag.

Schmidt-Brummer, H., and Lee, F. 1973. *Die Bemalte Stadt*. Berlin: Du Mont Buchverlag.

Serota, N.; Cork, R.; Tisdall, C.; et al. 1978. *Art for Society: Contemporary British Art with a Social or Political Purpose*. London: Whitechapel Art Gallery.

(Seymour, D.) 1986. *Dermot Seymour* (in conversation with N. Speers and introduction by D. Healy). Exhibition catalog. Belfast: Fenderesky Art Gallery.

Shaw, F. 1972. "The Canon of Irish History: A Challenge." *Studies* (summer).

Simpson, E. 1980. "Chicano Street Murals: A Sociological Perspective." *Journal of Popular Culture* 13, part 3, pp. 516–25.

Sinn Féin. 1970. *Éire Nua*. Dublin.

Siqueiros, D. A. 1975. *Art and Revolution*. London: Lawrence and Wishart.

Smith, D. 1983. *Irish Republican Images*. Catalog of mixed media exhibition. London: Pentonville Gallery, November/December.

Sommer, R. 1975. *Street Art*. New York: Links Books.

Sontag, S. 1970. "Posters: Advertisement, Art, Political Artifact, Commodity". In *The Art of Revolution, Stermer, D.,* pp. vii–xxiii. New York: McGraw Hill.

Stermer, D. 1970. *The Art of Revolution*. New York: McGraw-Hill.

Thalacker, D. 1980. *The Place of Art in the World of Architecture*. New York: Chelsea House Publishers.

Tomlinson, M. 1980. "Relegating Local Government." In *Northern Ireland: Between Civil Rights and Civil War*, L. O'Dowd, B. Rolston and M. Tomlinson, pp. 95–118. London: CSE Books.

Trotsky, L. 1975. *Culture and Socialism*. London: New Park Publications.

Velez, J. 1964. "The Art of Illegal Propaganda." *World Marxist Review* 7, part 9, pp. 47–50.

Vicuna, C. 1974. "The Coup came to kill what I Loved". *Spare Rib* 28: pp. 36–38.

Walker, G. 1985. *The Politics of Frustration*. Manchester: Manchester University Press.

Walker, U. 1985. "Communicating with Itself." *Artists' Newsletter*, December, pp. 26–27.

Waller, J. 1987. "Nicaraguan Dawn." In *Strong Voices: Culture and Democracy in Chile and Nicaragua*. West Bromwich: Another Standard, pp. 6–10.

Watson, J. 1983. "Brightening the Place up?" *Circa* 8 (January/February), pp. 4–10.

Wilson, D. 1983. "The Painted Message." *Circa* 8 (January/February), pp. 19–20.

Young Unionist Council. 1986. *Cuchulain: The Lost Legend*. Belfast.

Subject Index

References to illustrations are in boldface type. All places referred to are in Belfast, unless otherwise stated. All mural artists referred to are from Northern Ireland, unless otherwise stated.

Author Index